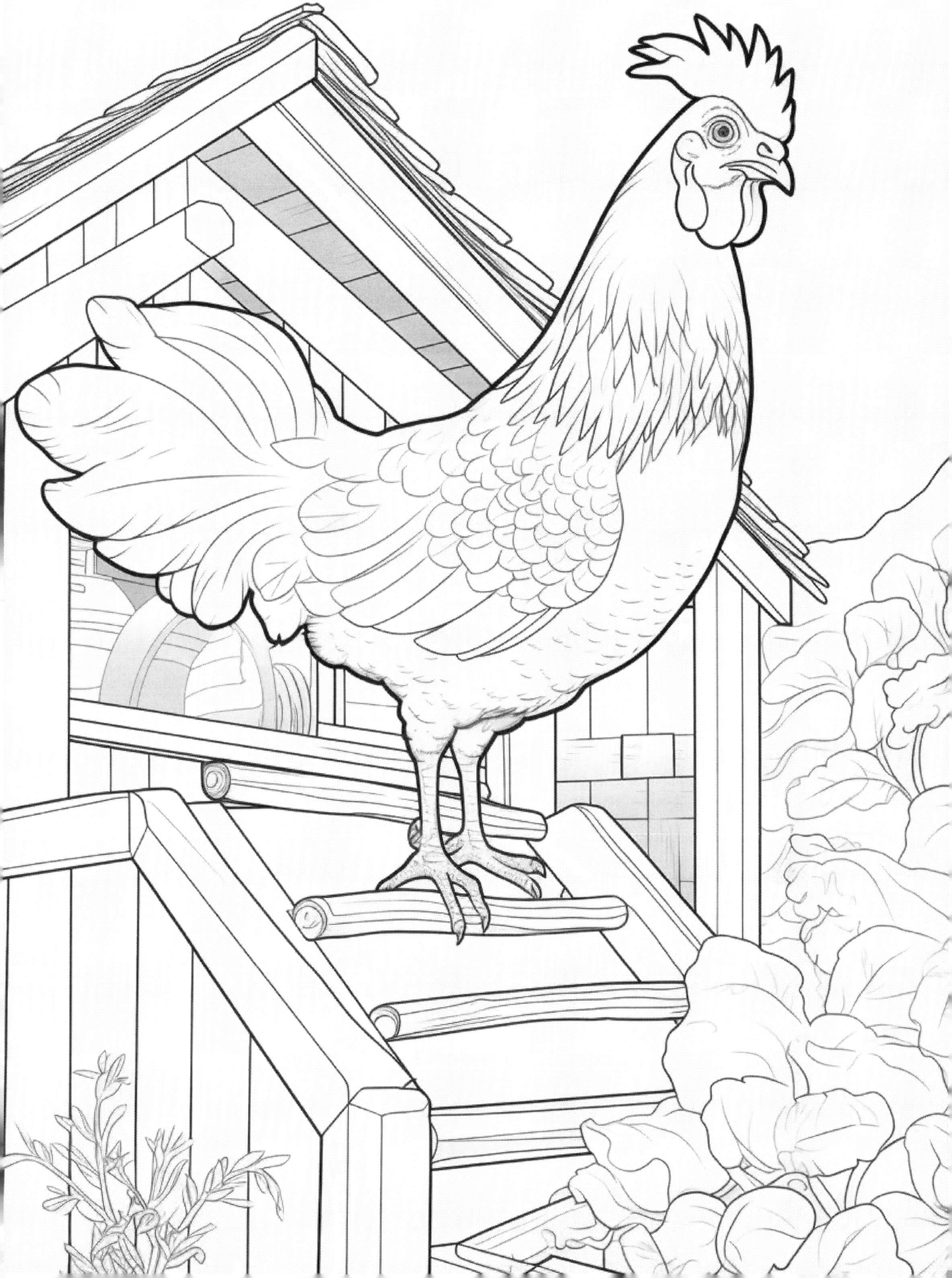

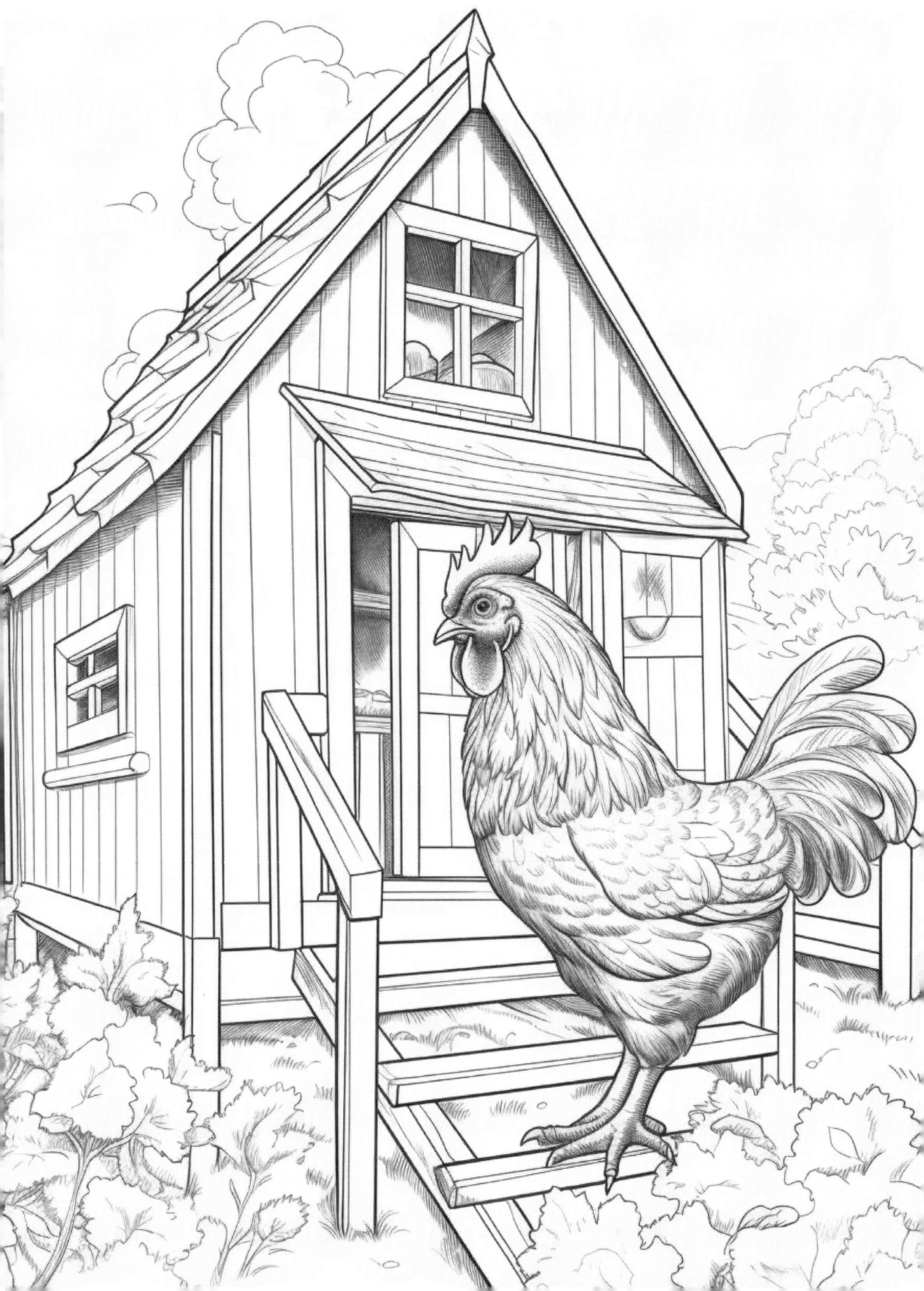

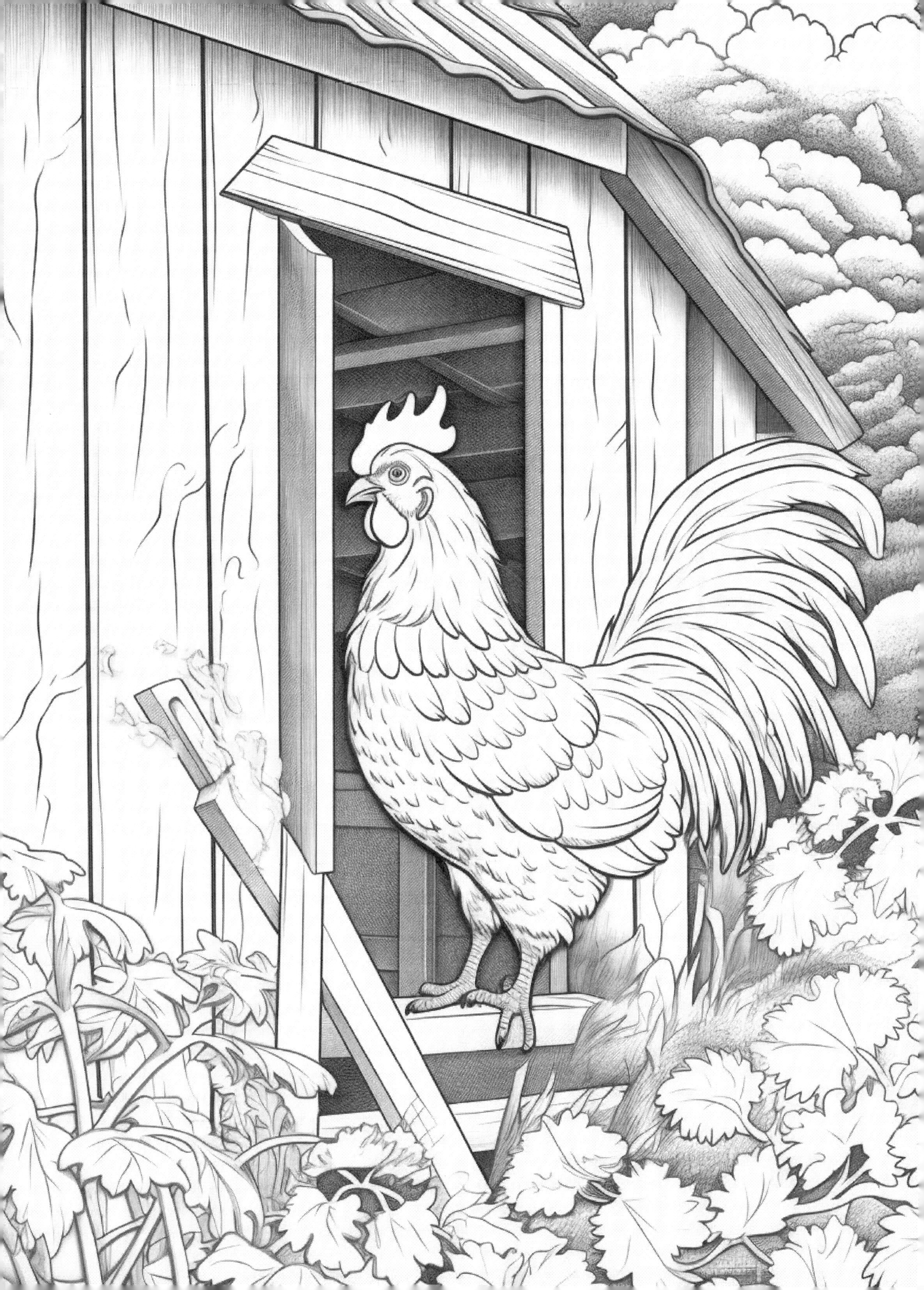

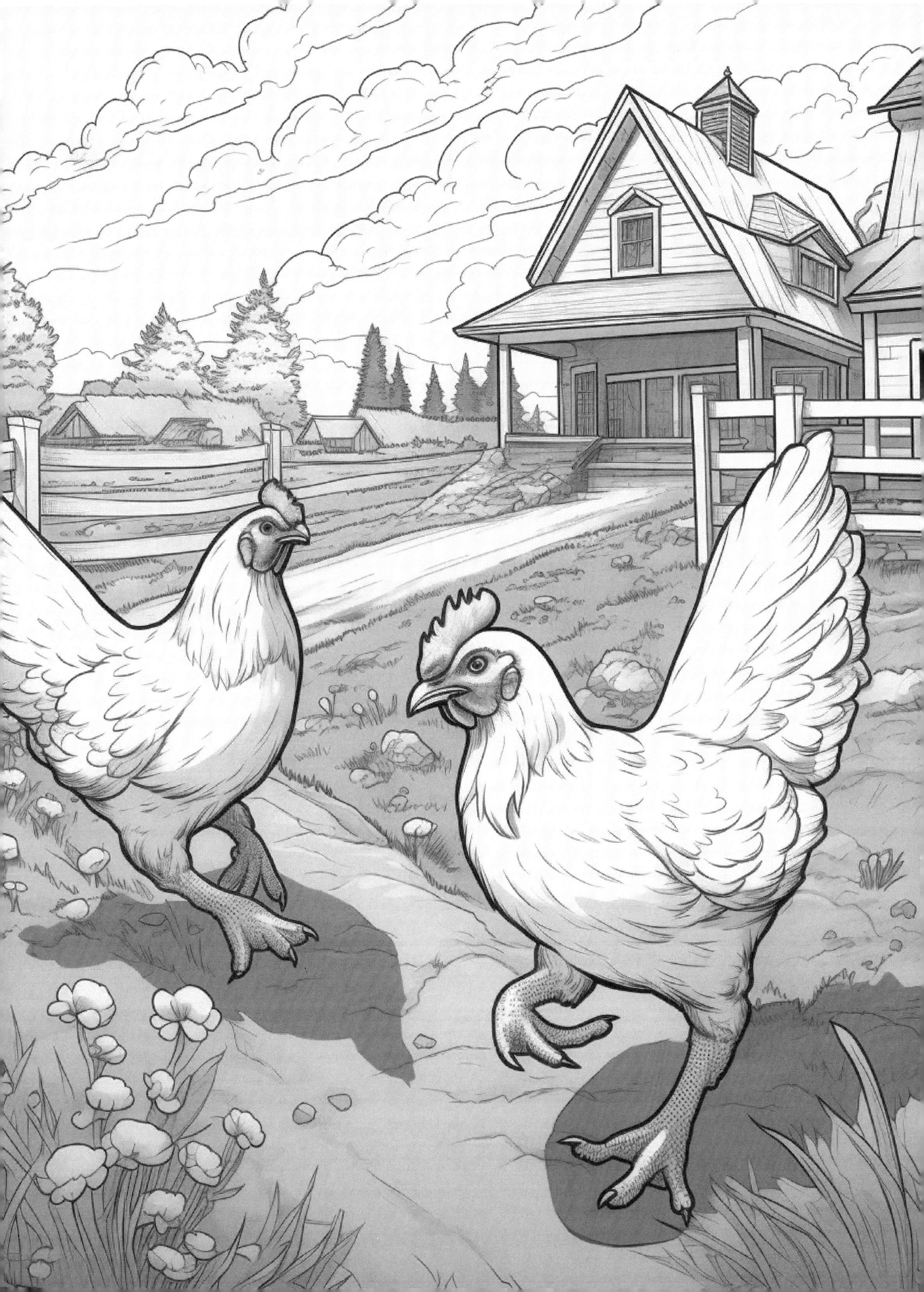

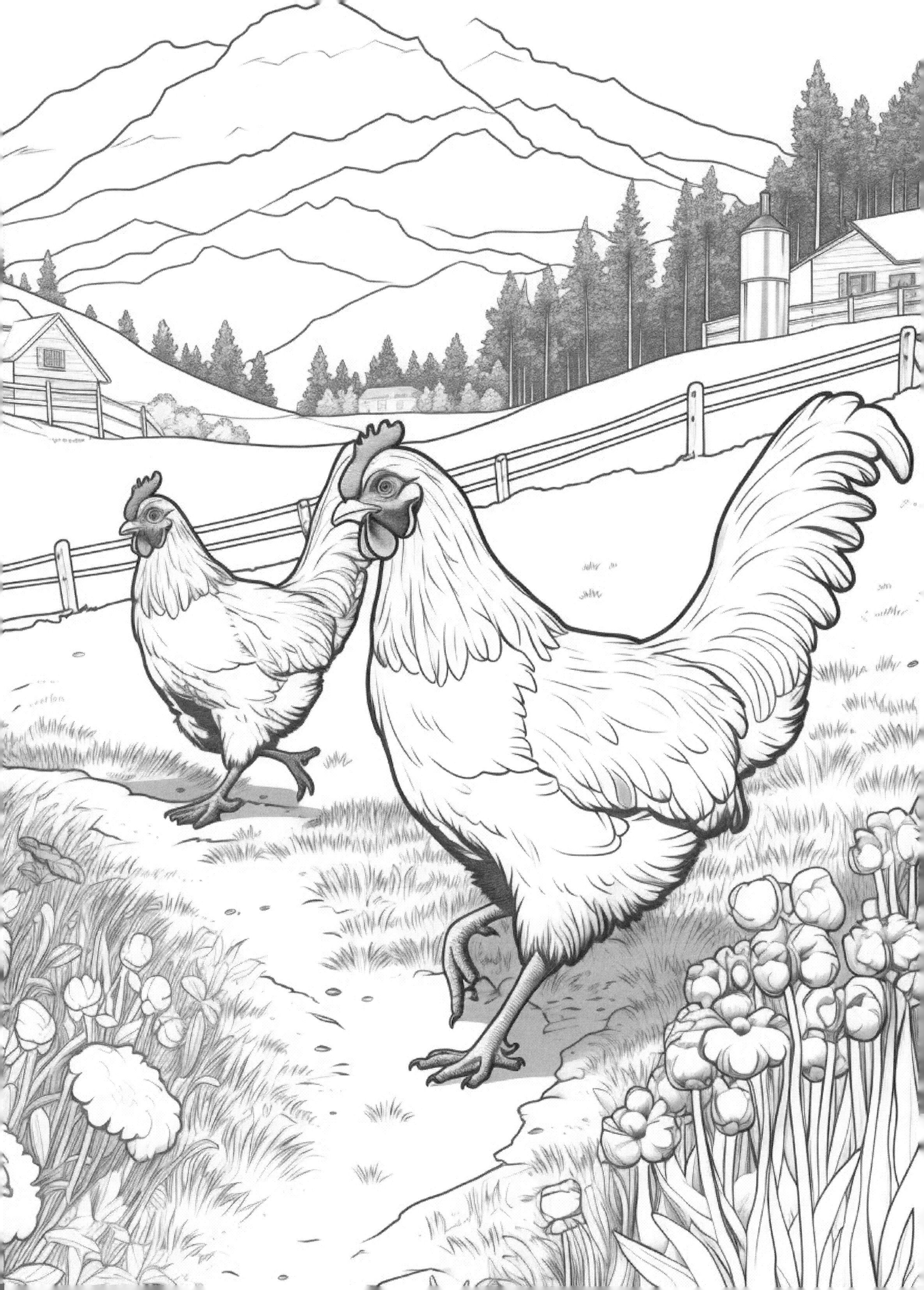

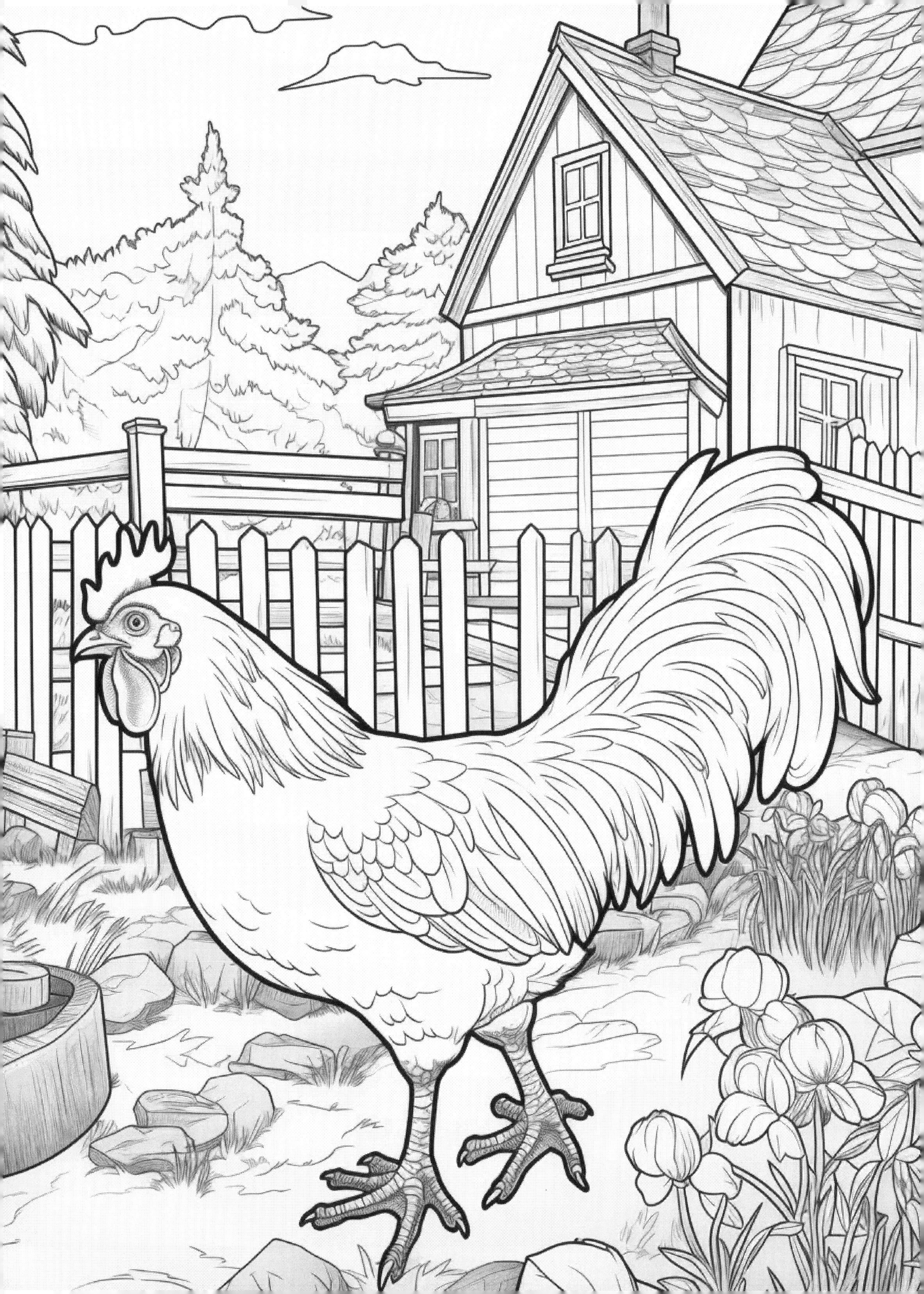

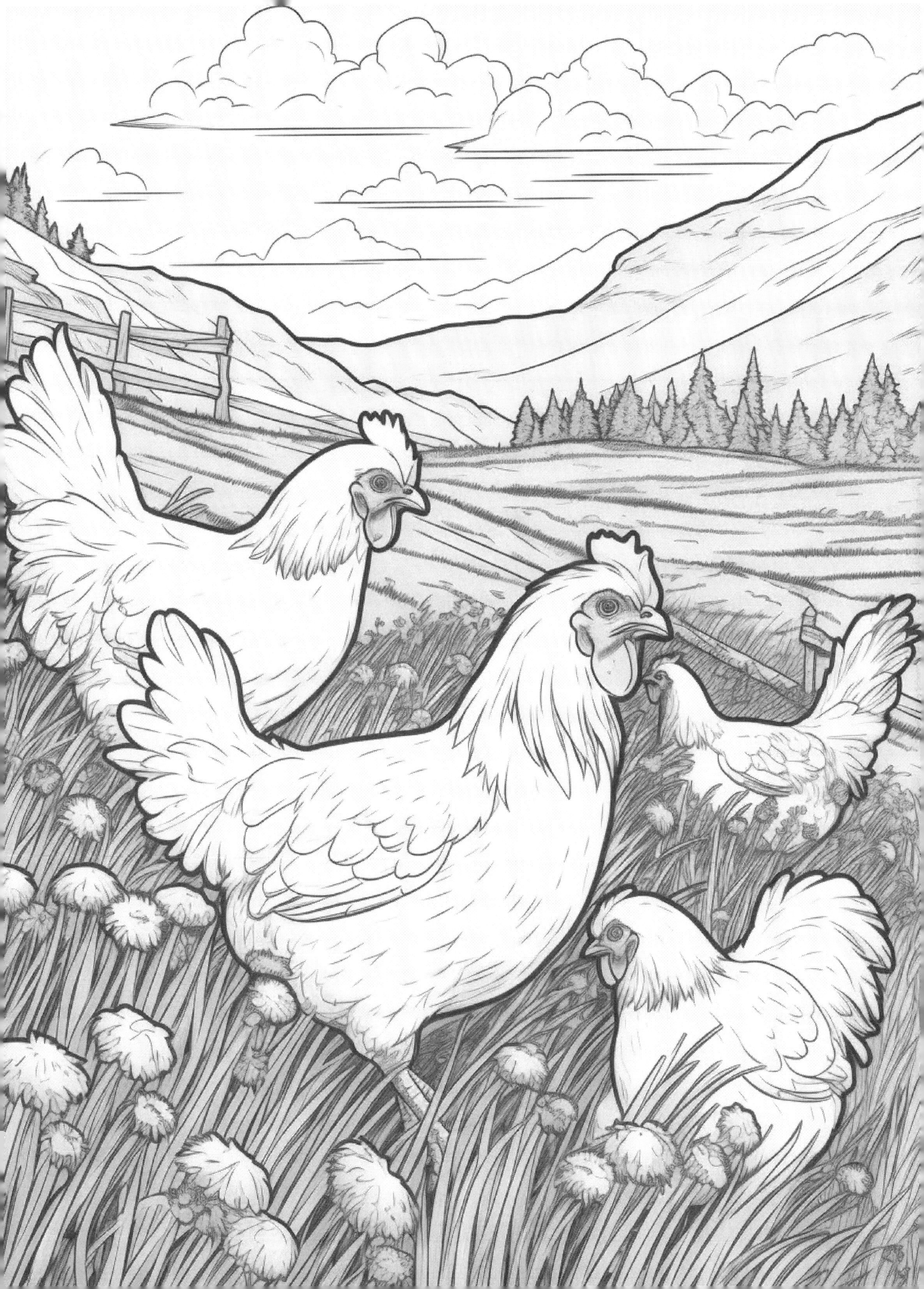

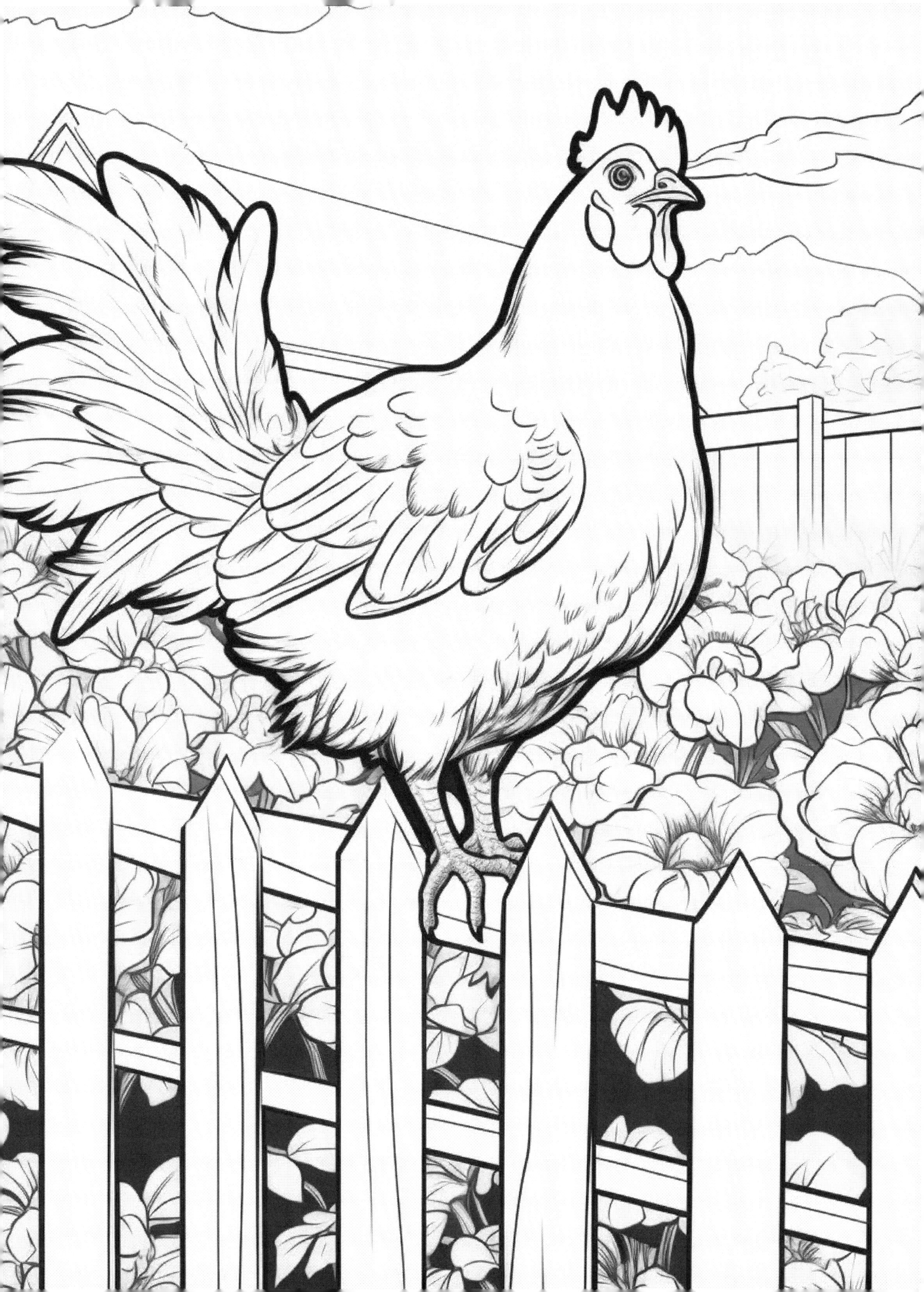

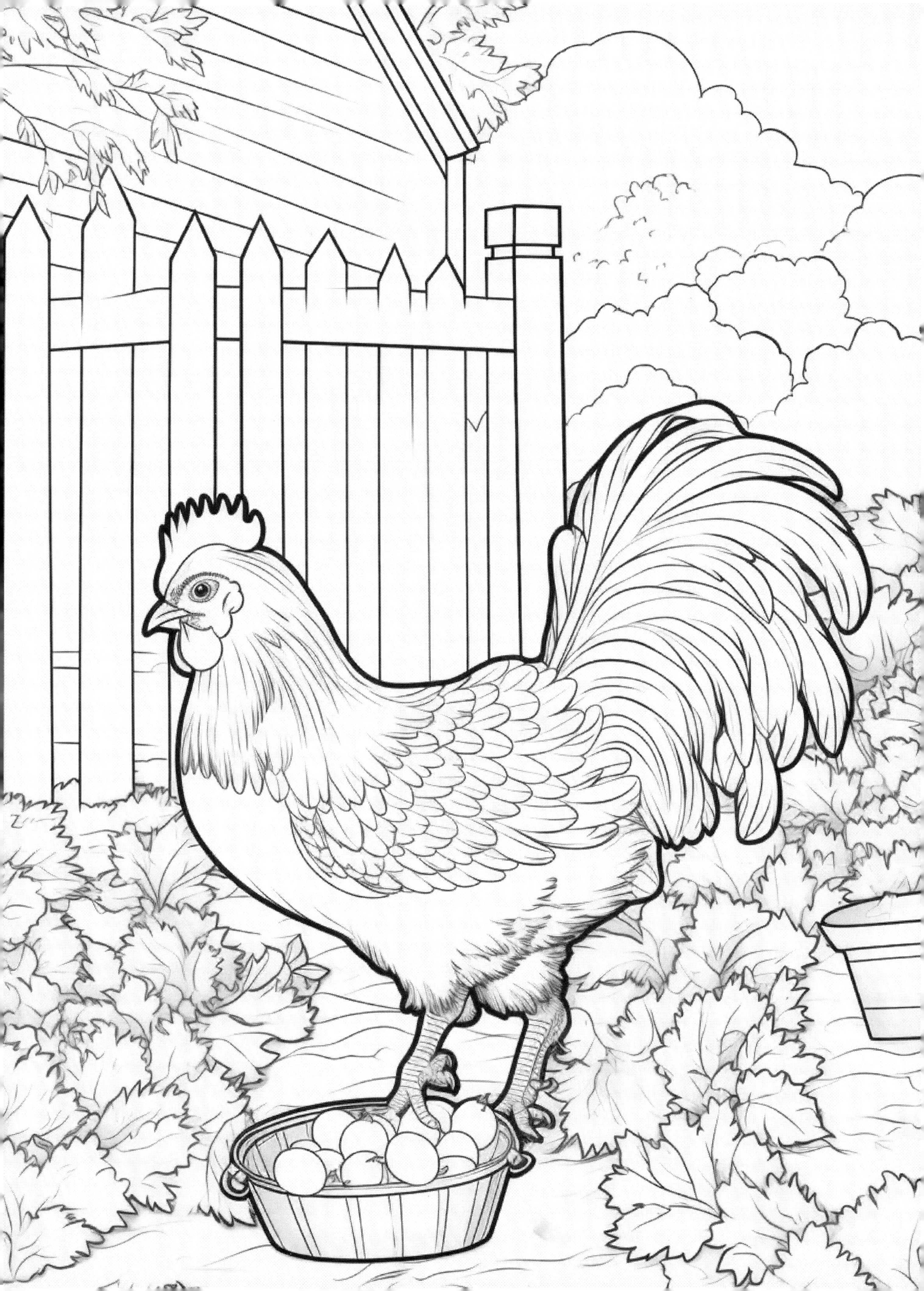

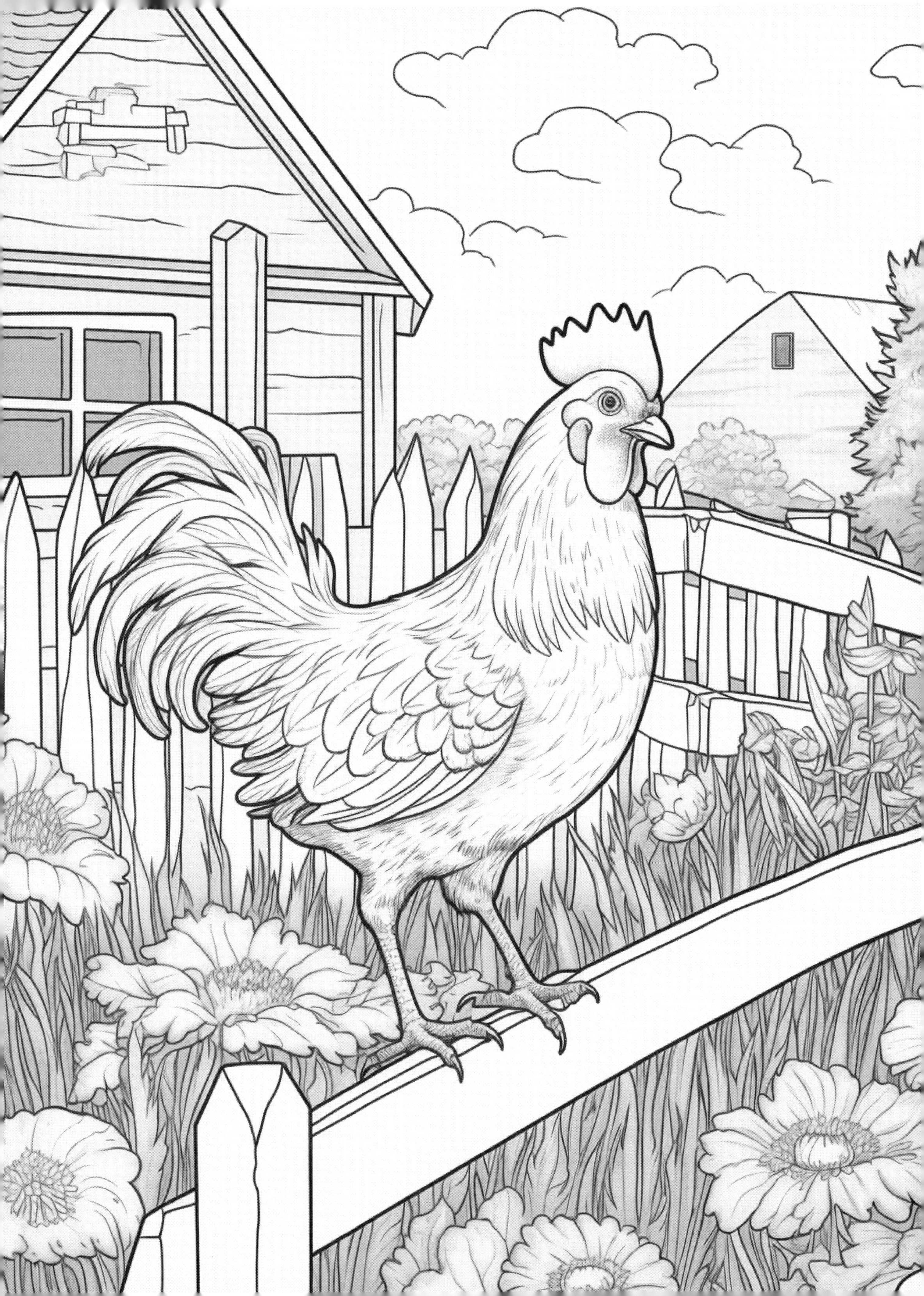

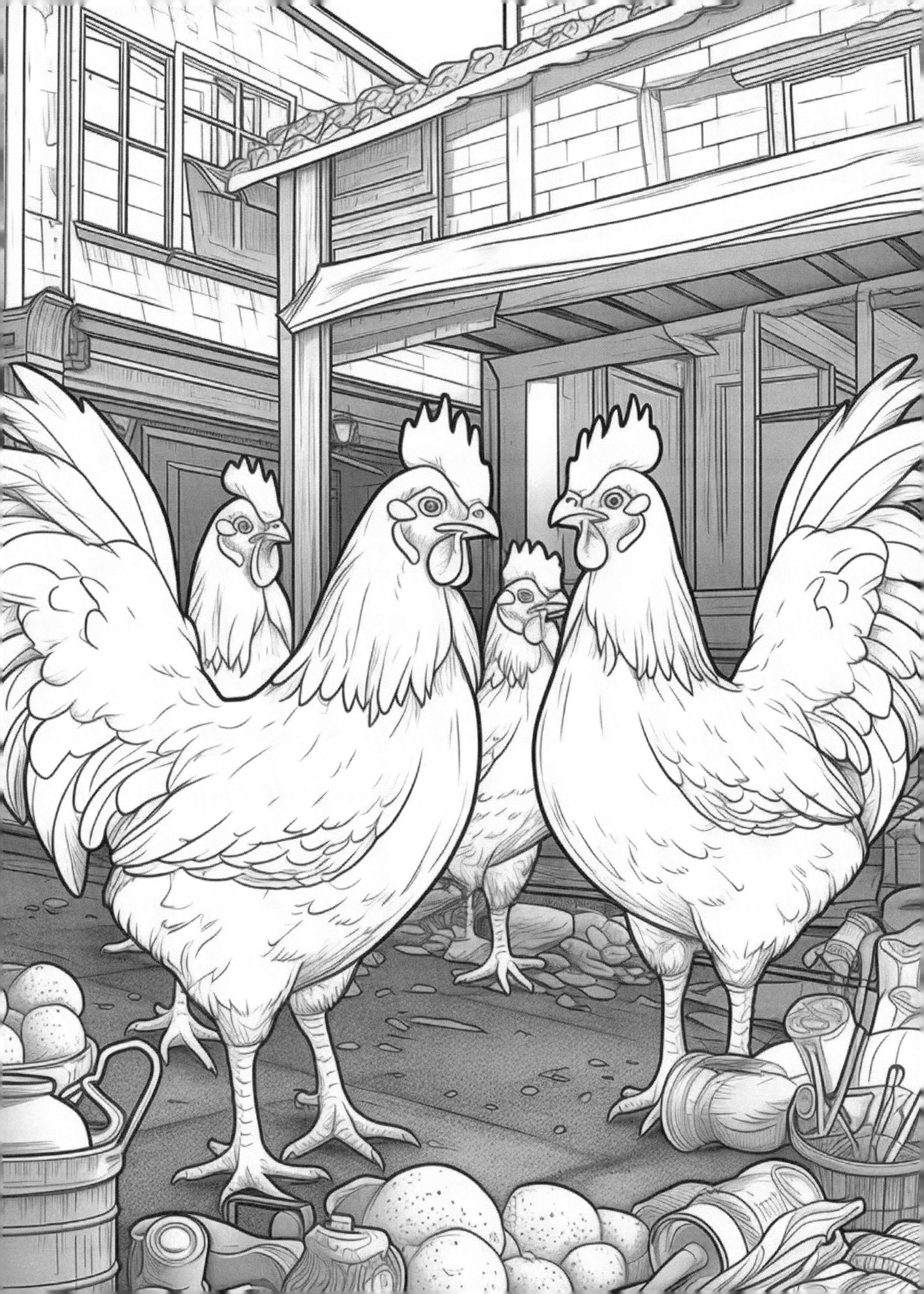

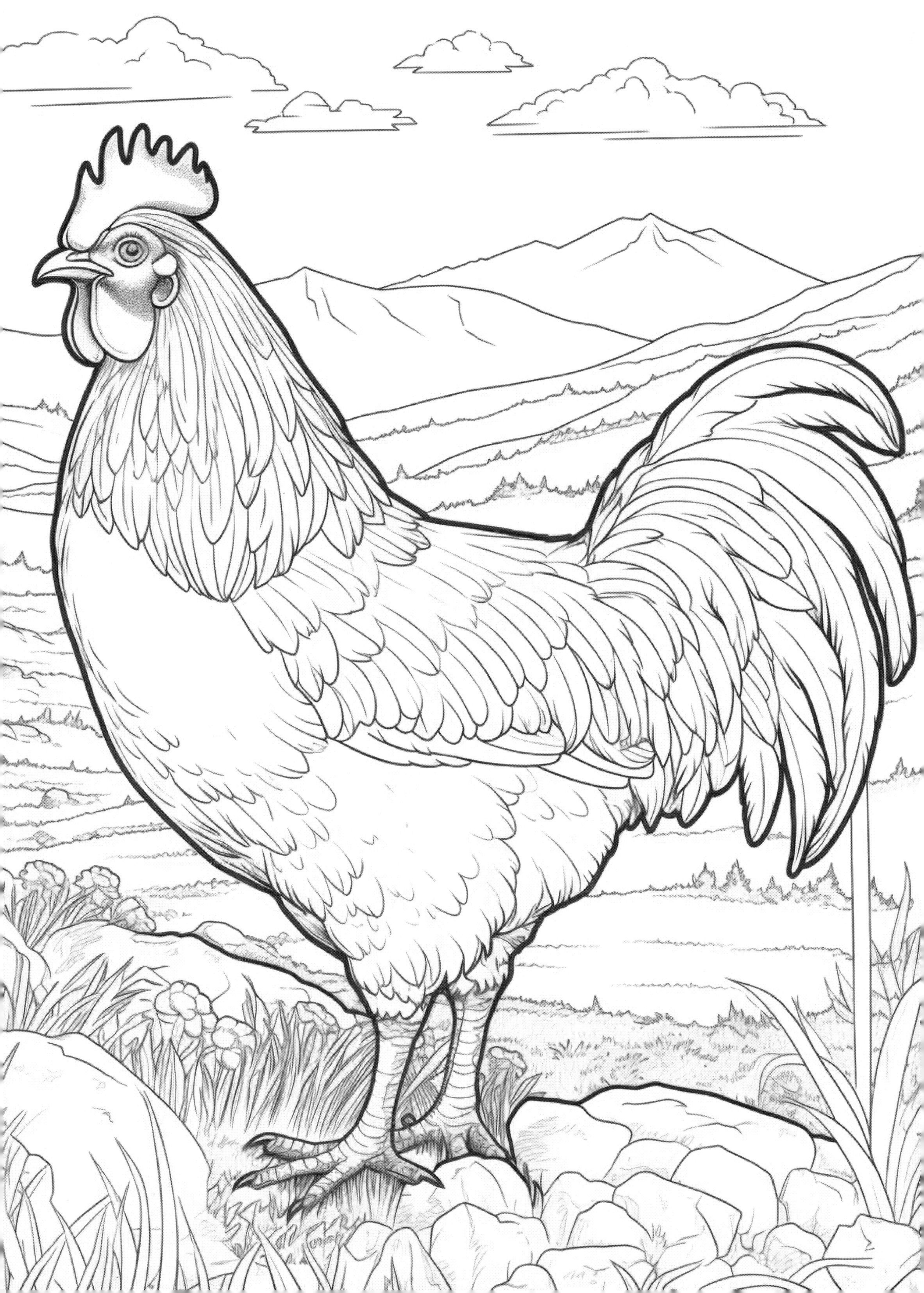

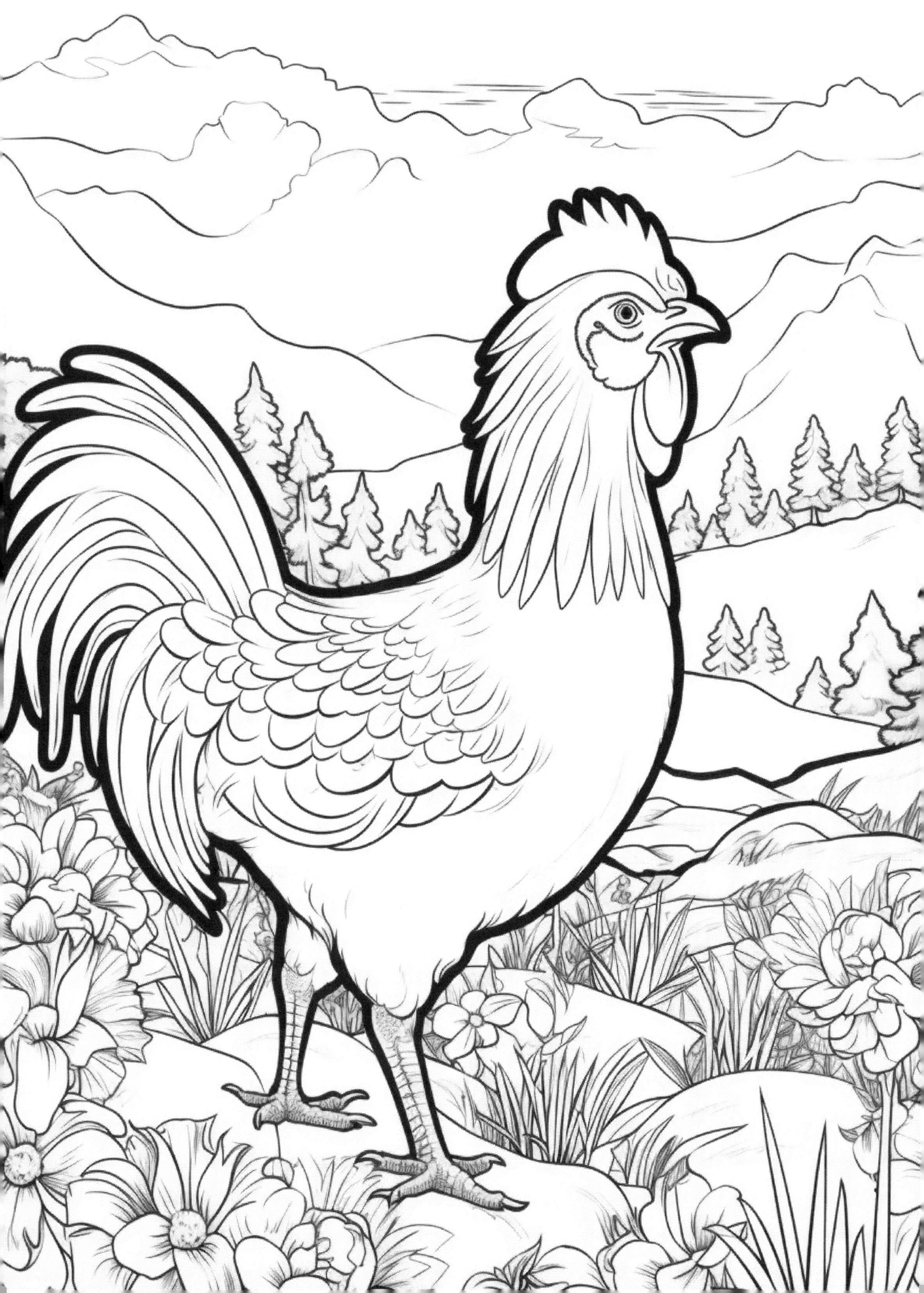

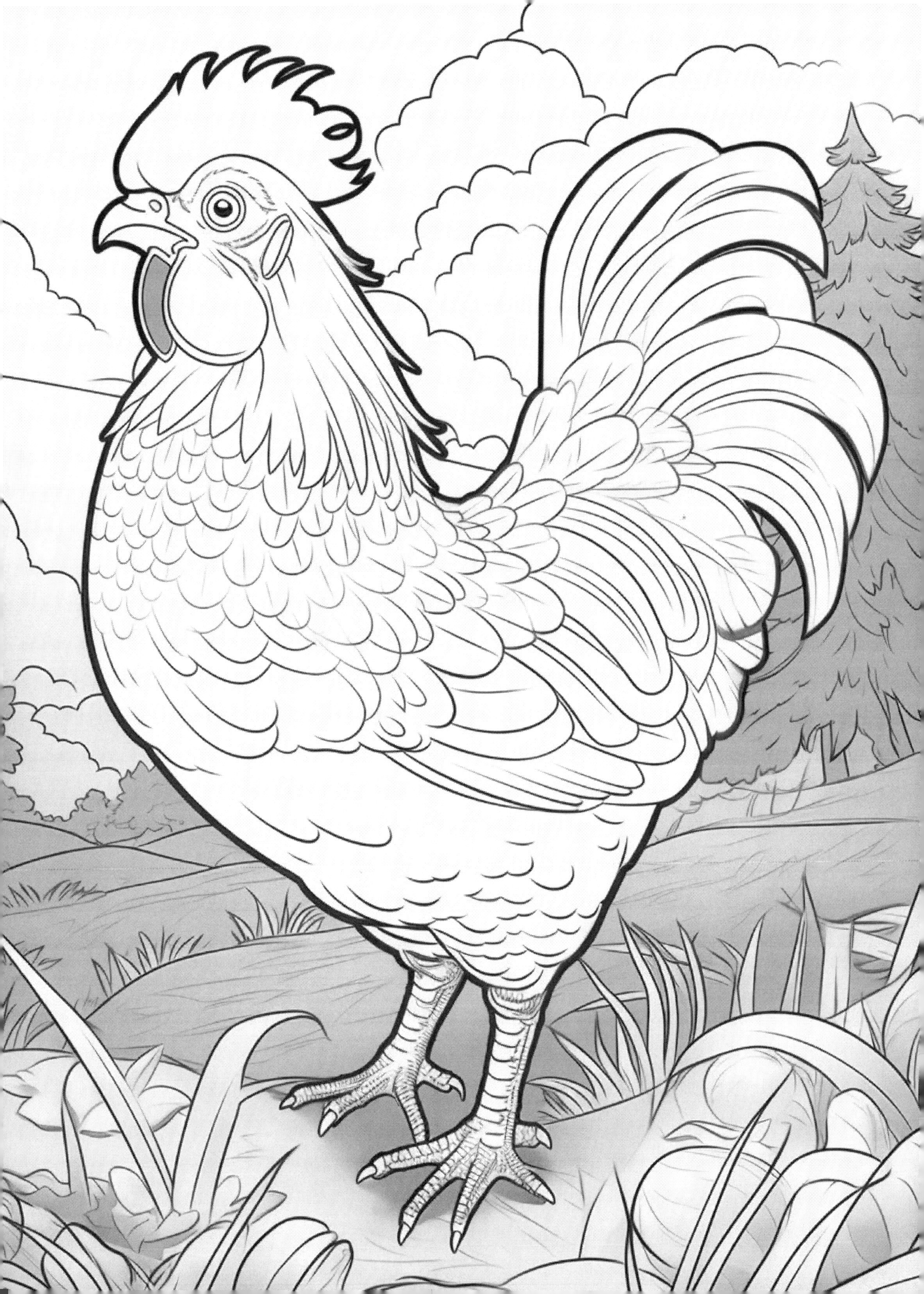

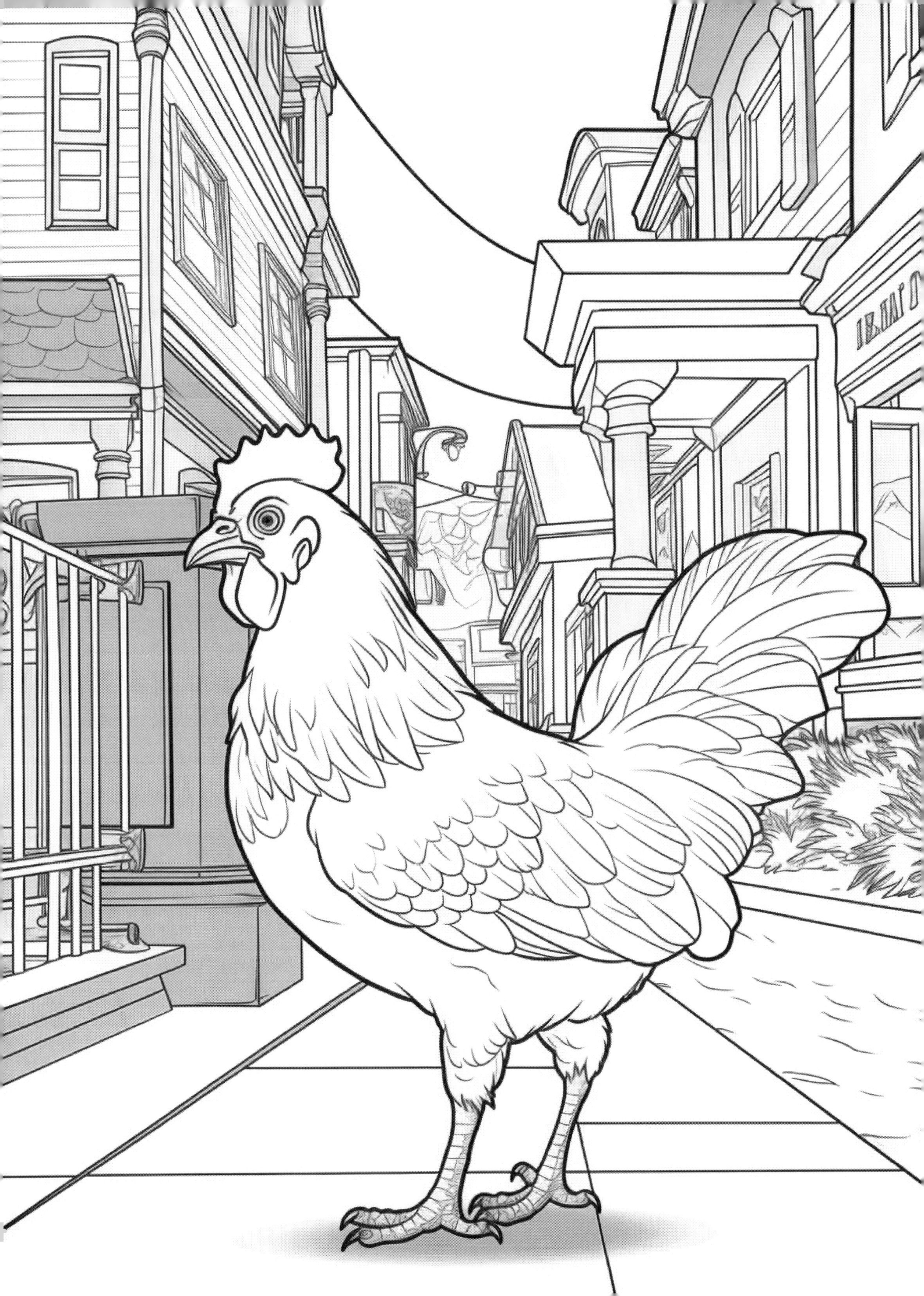

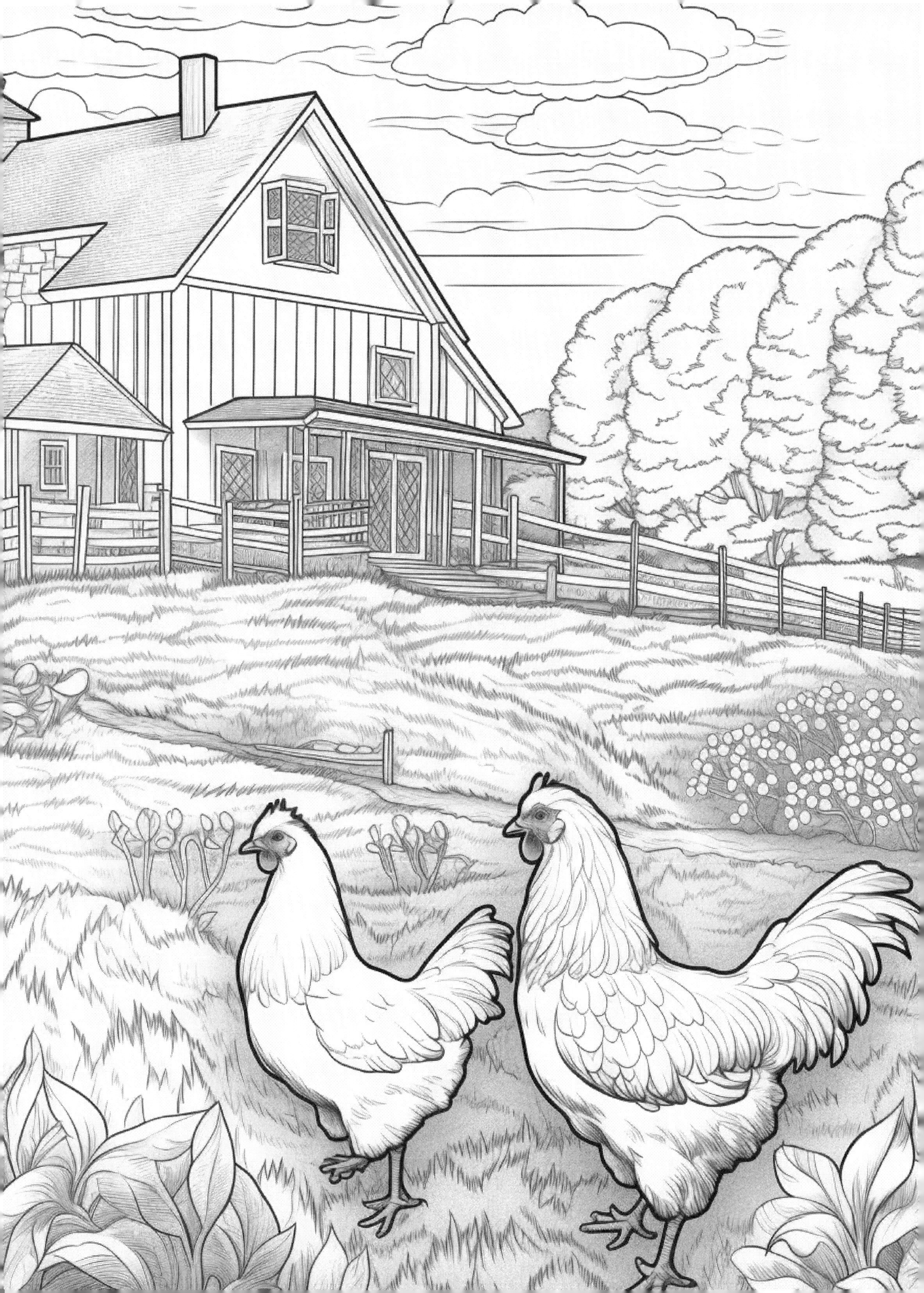

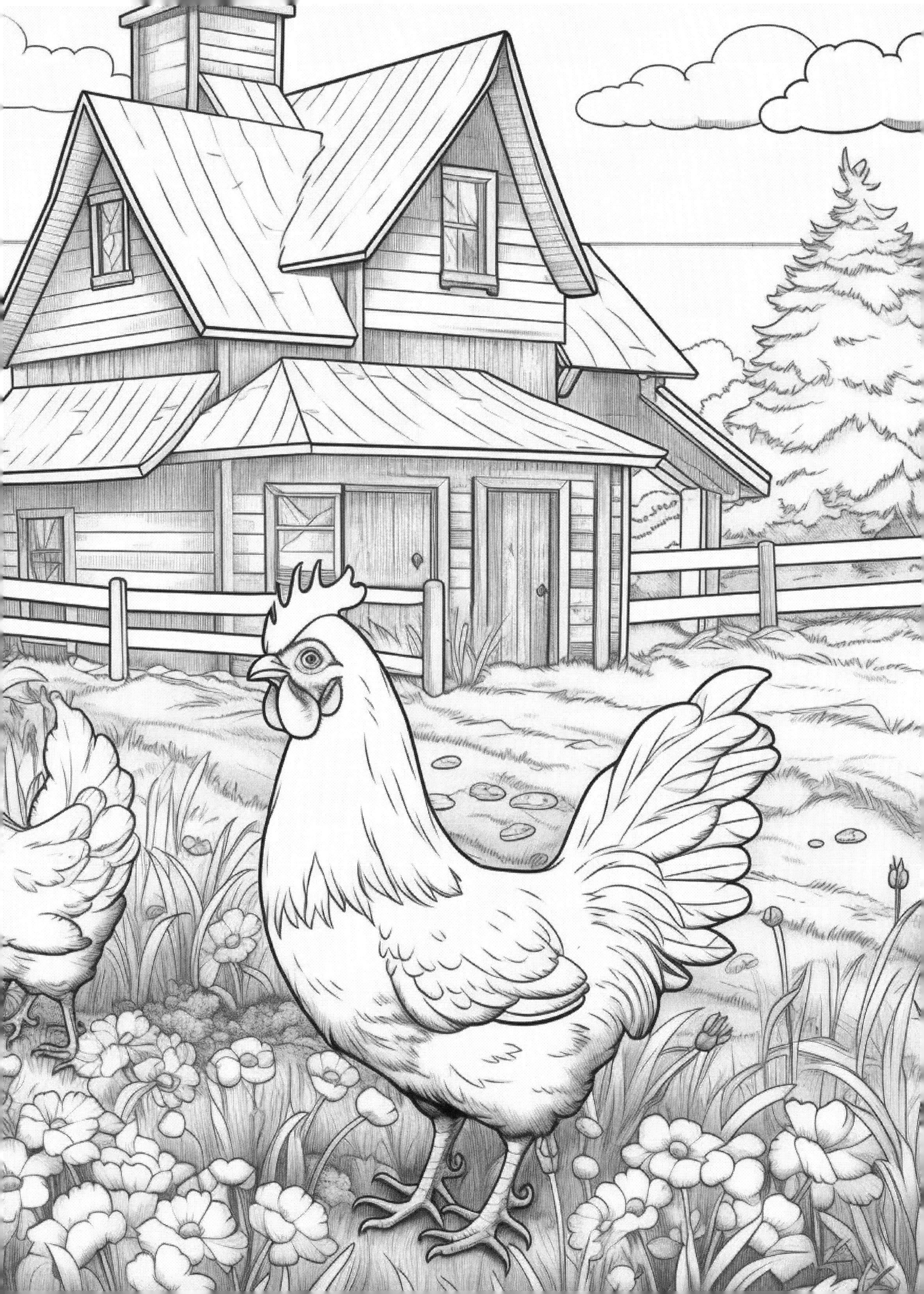

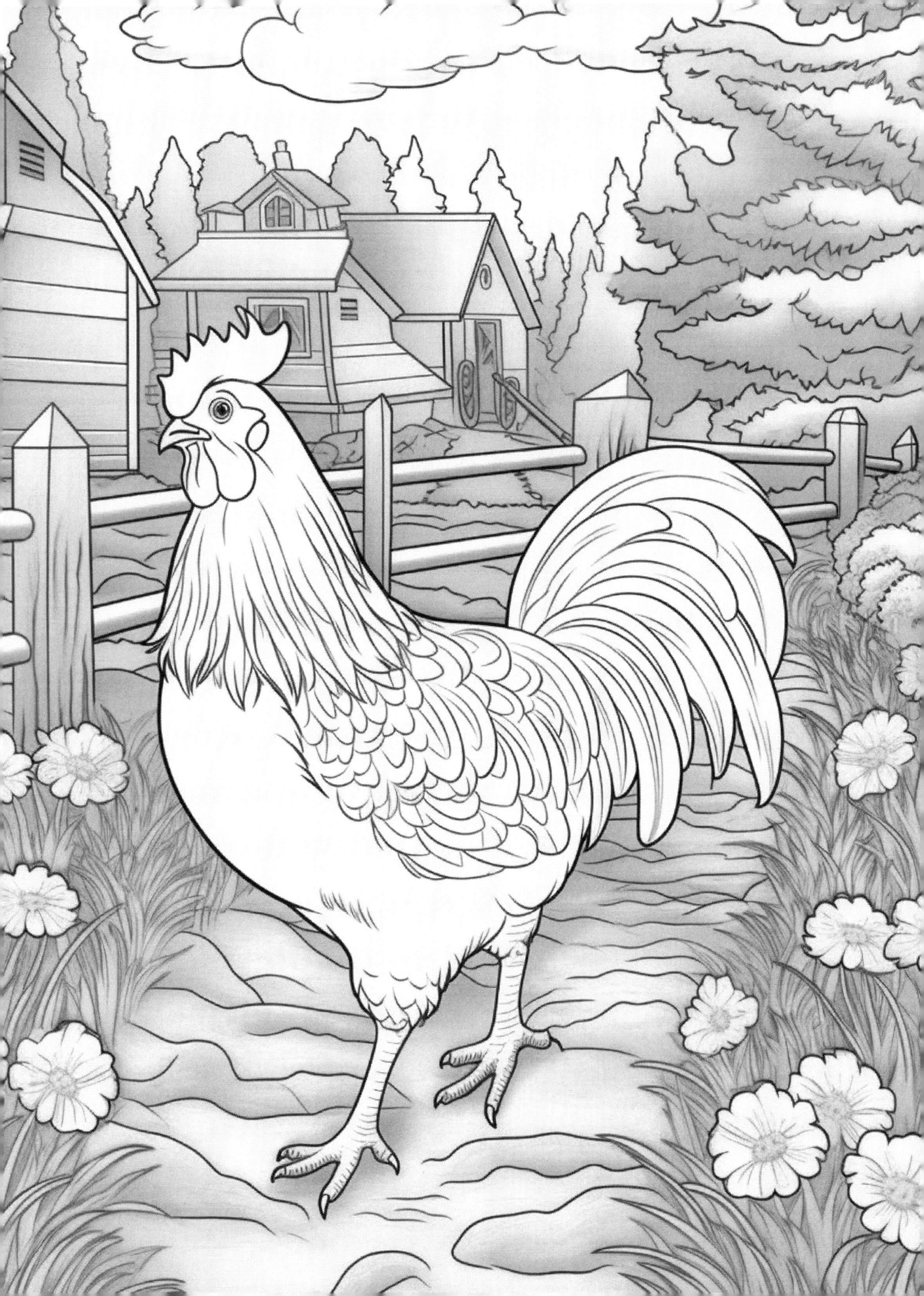

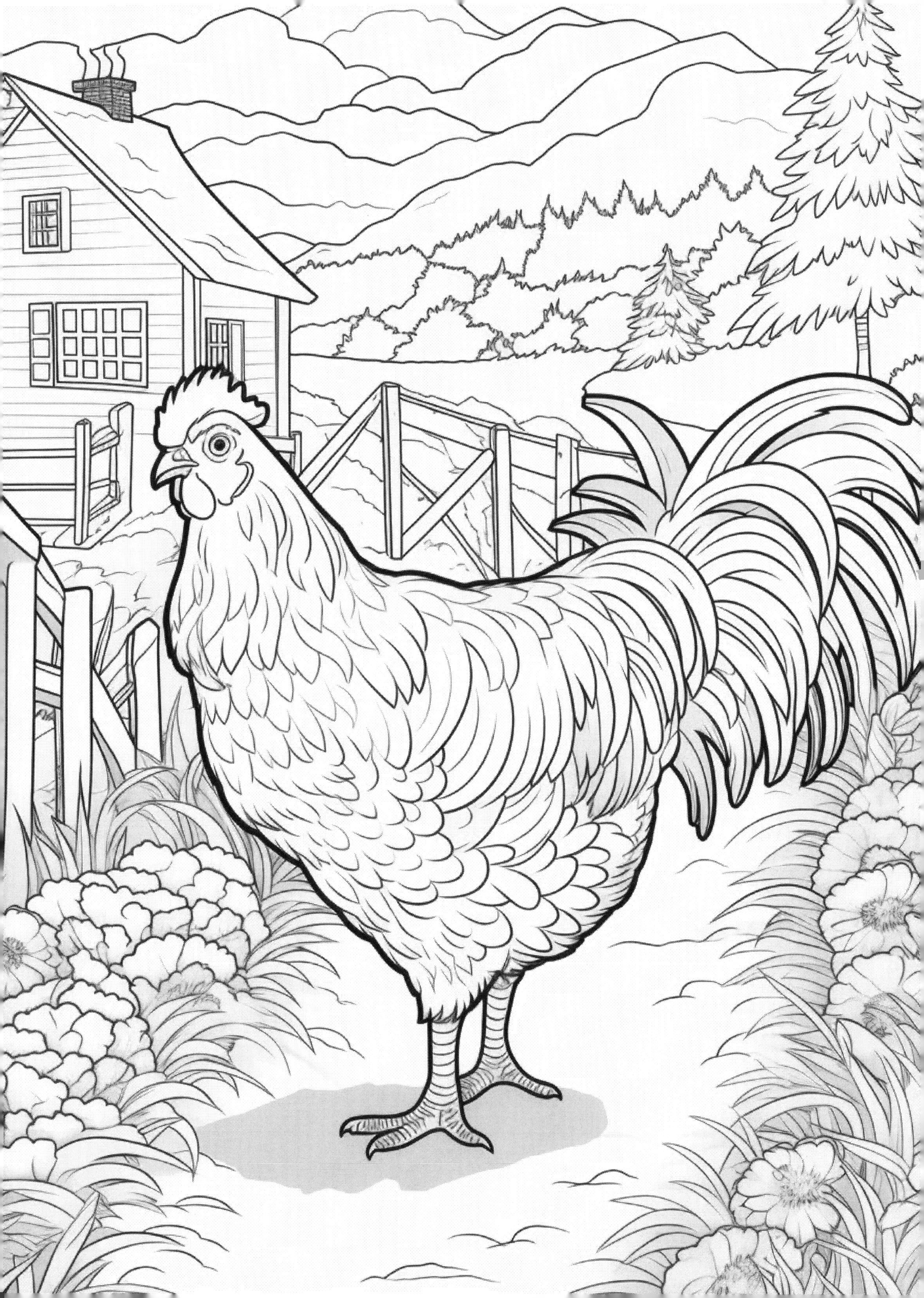

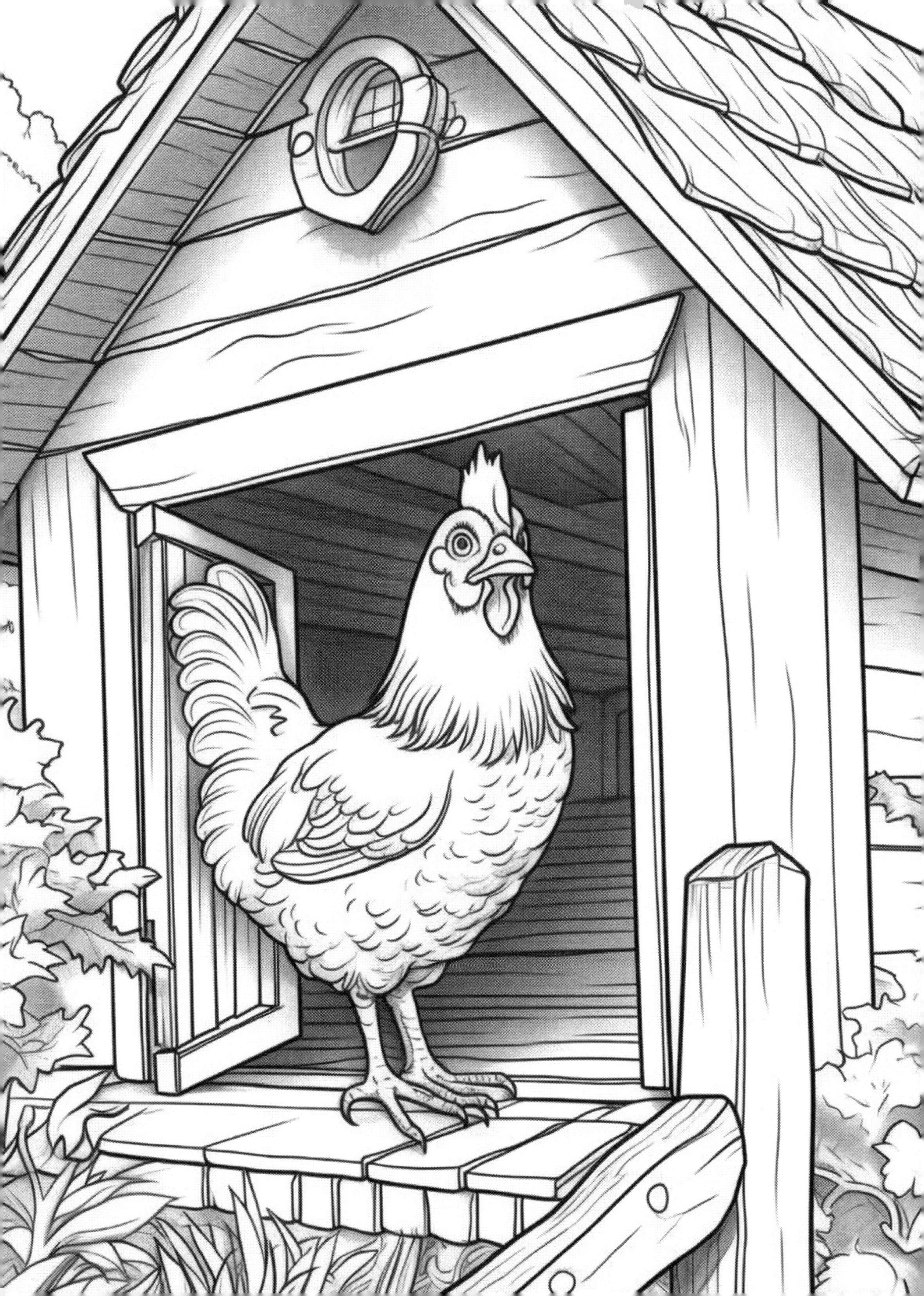

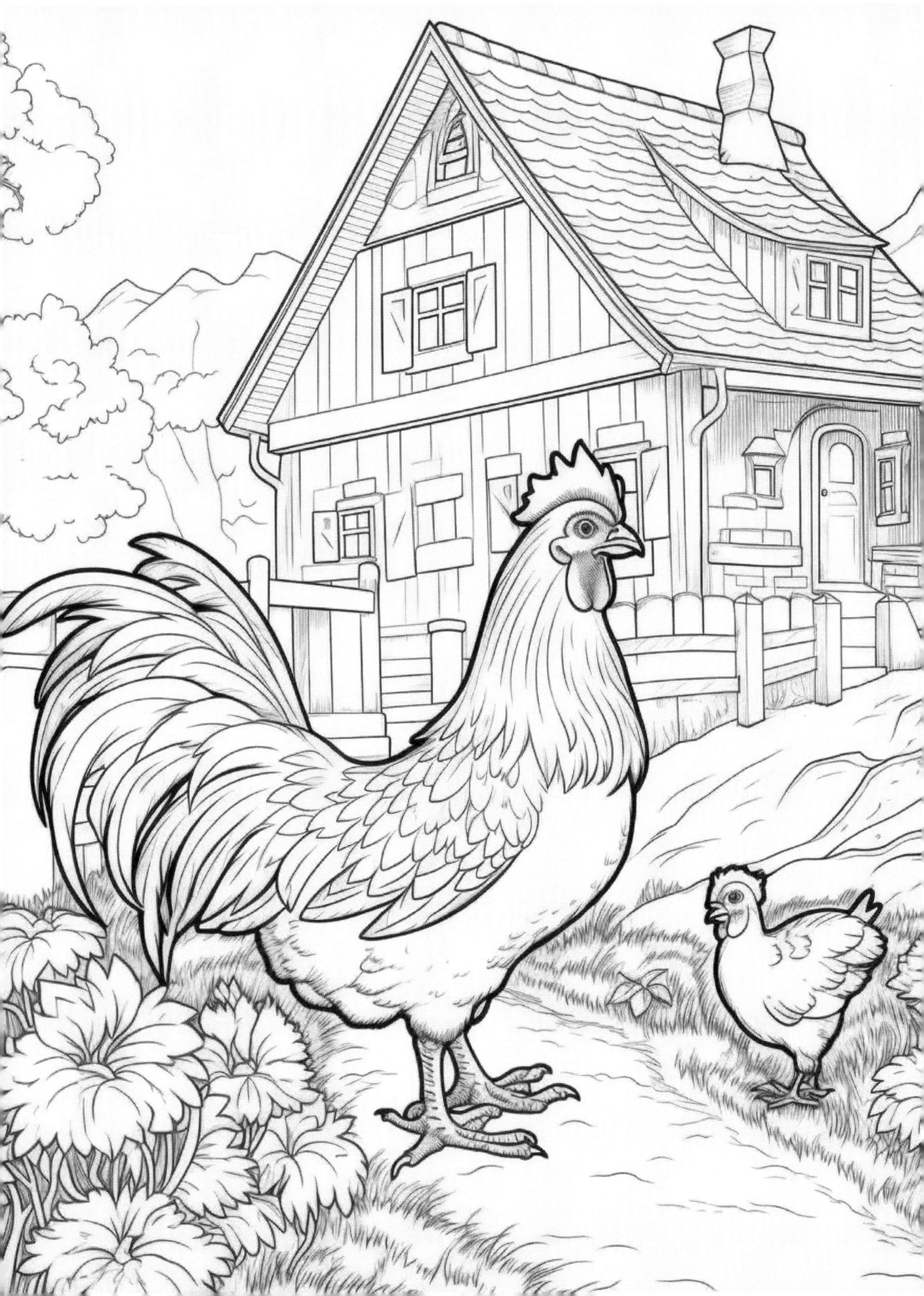

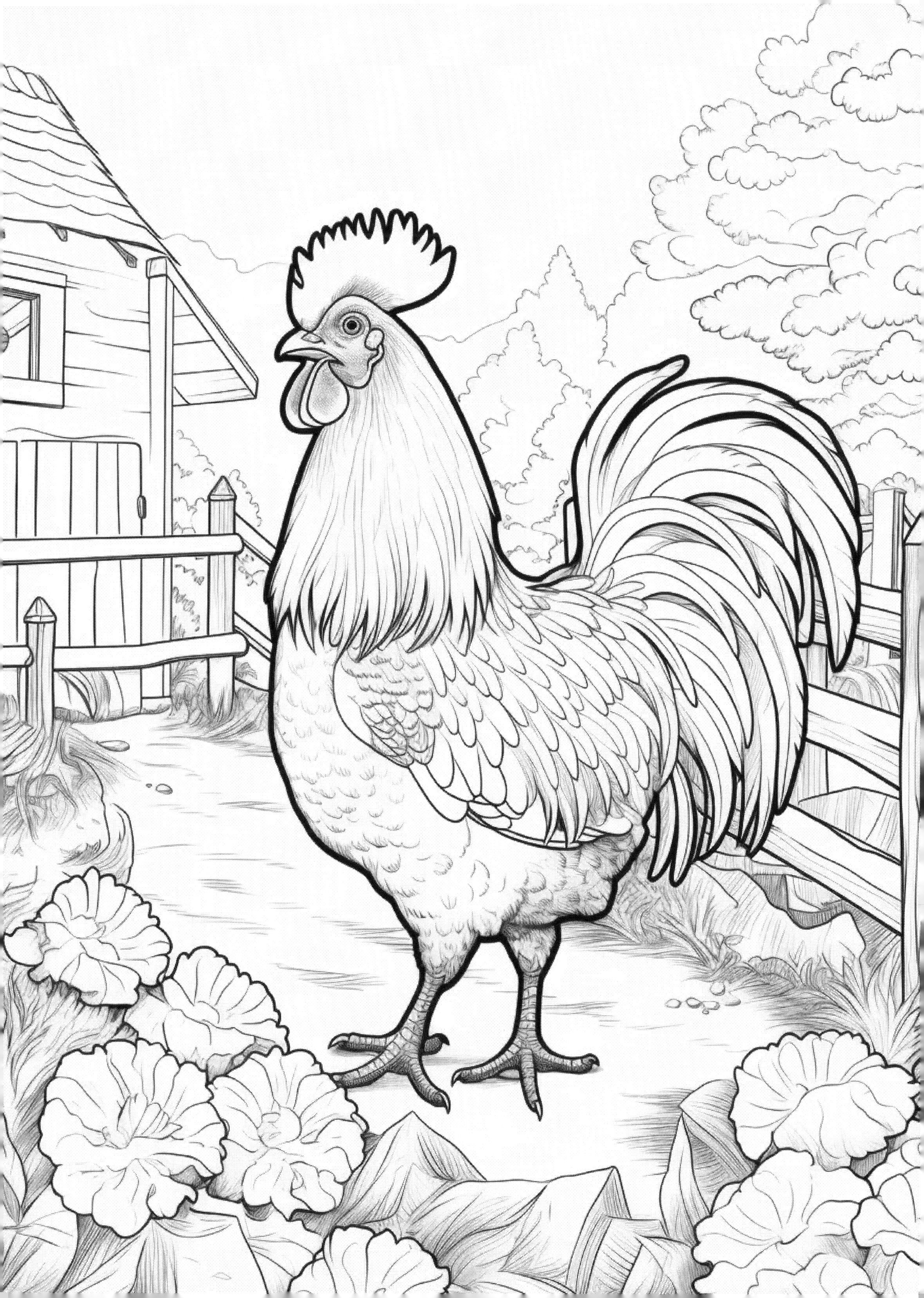

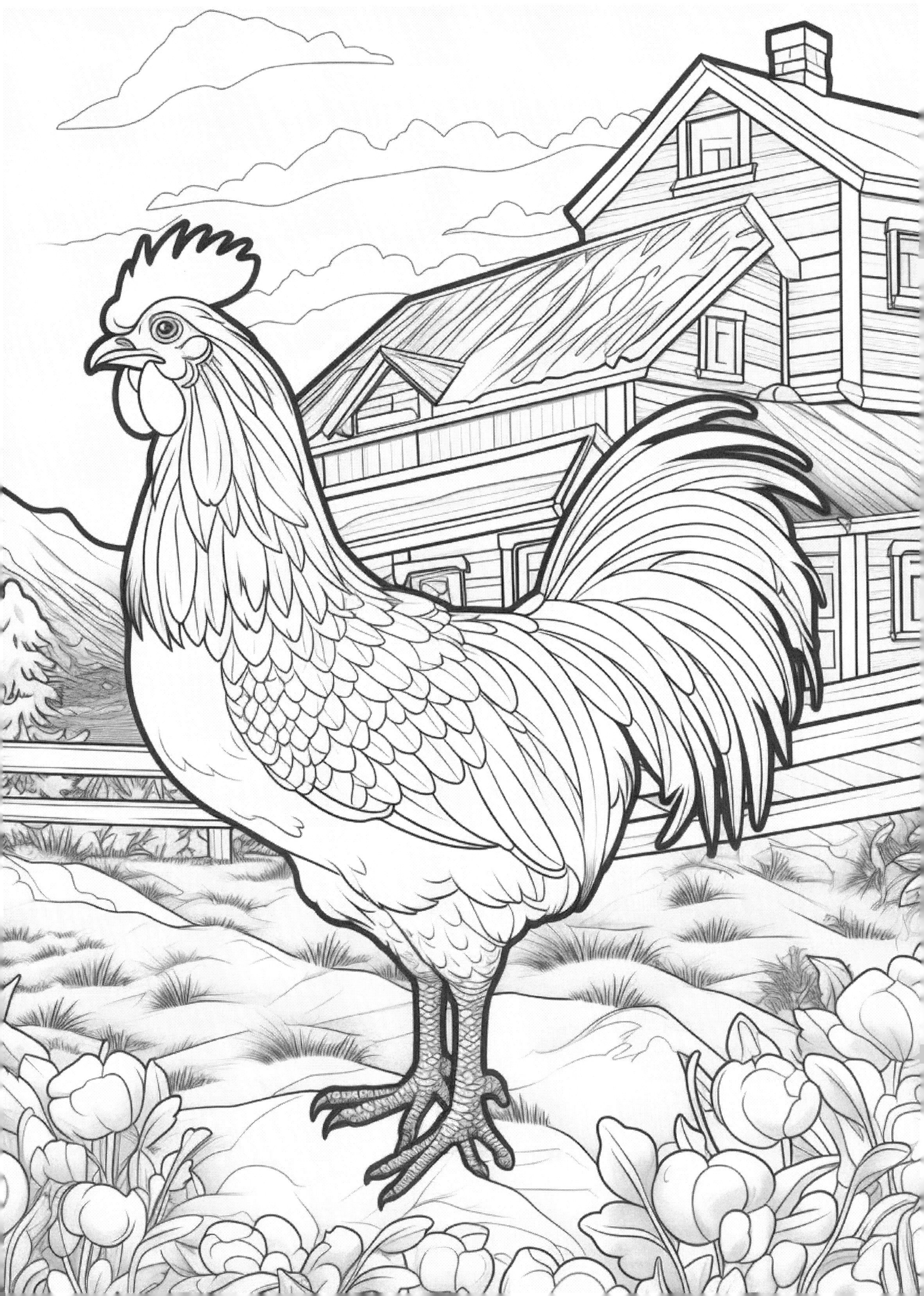

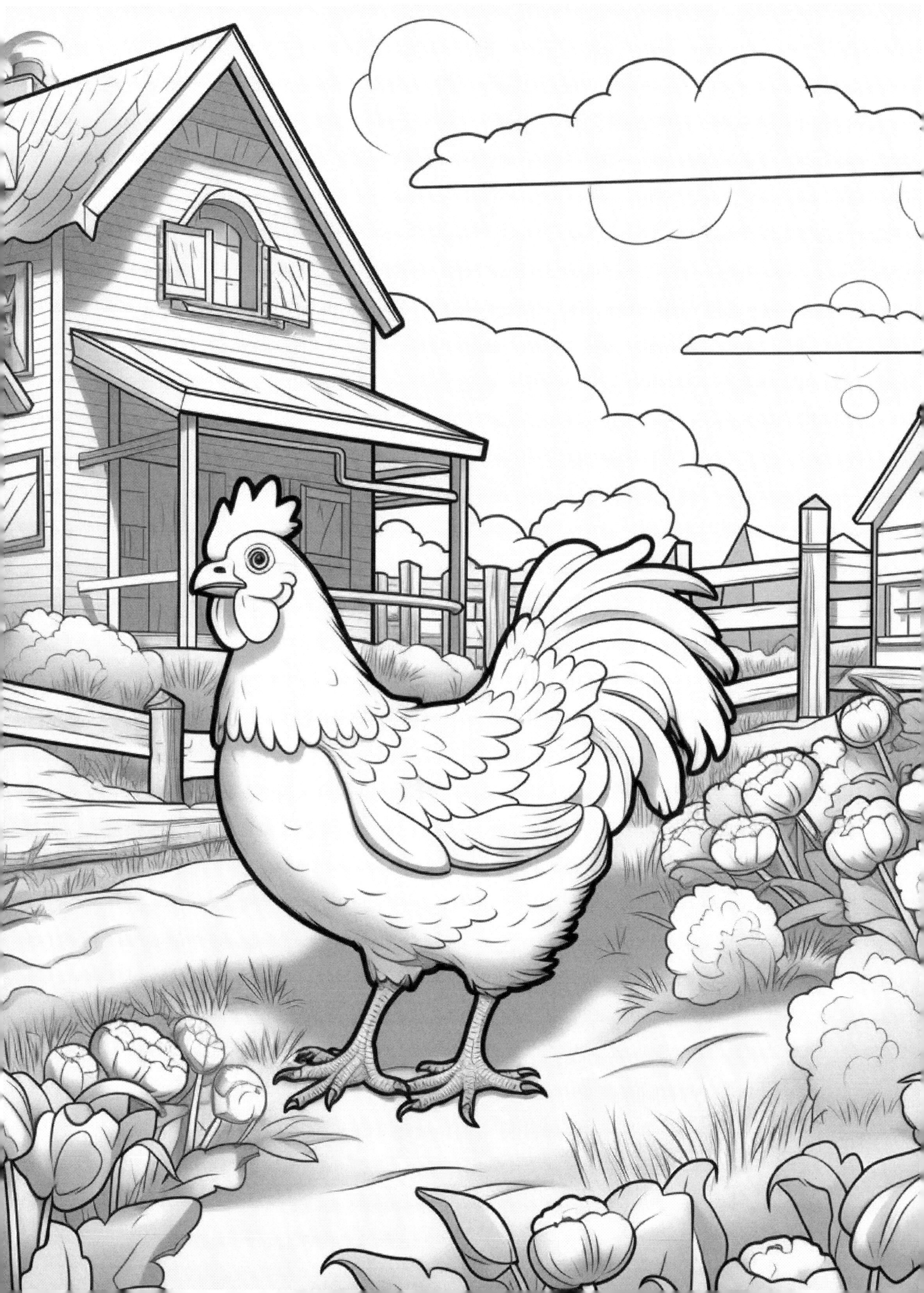

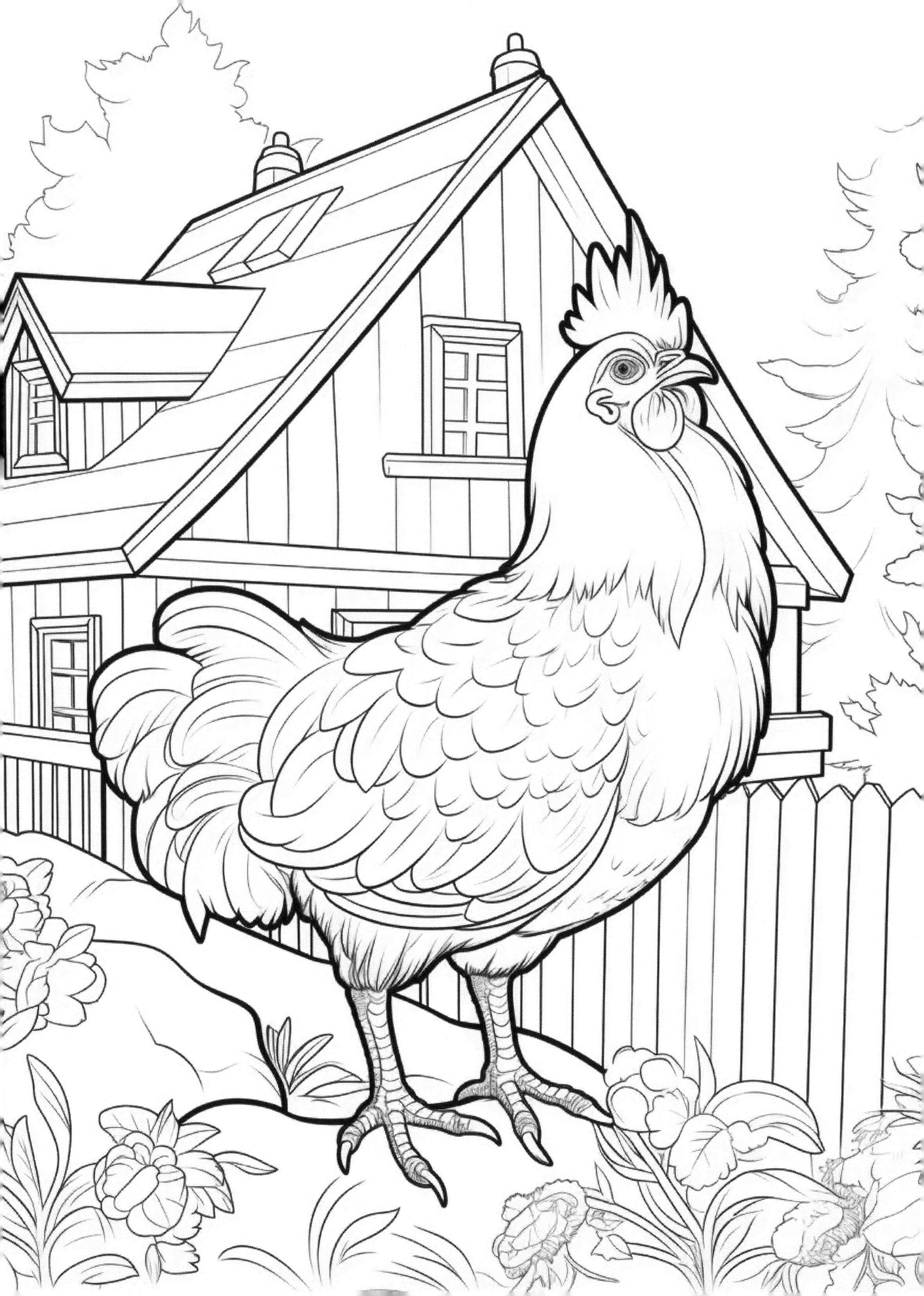

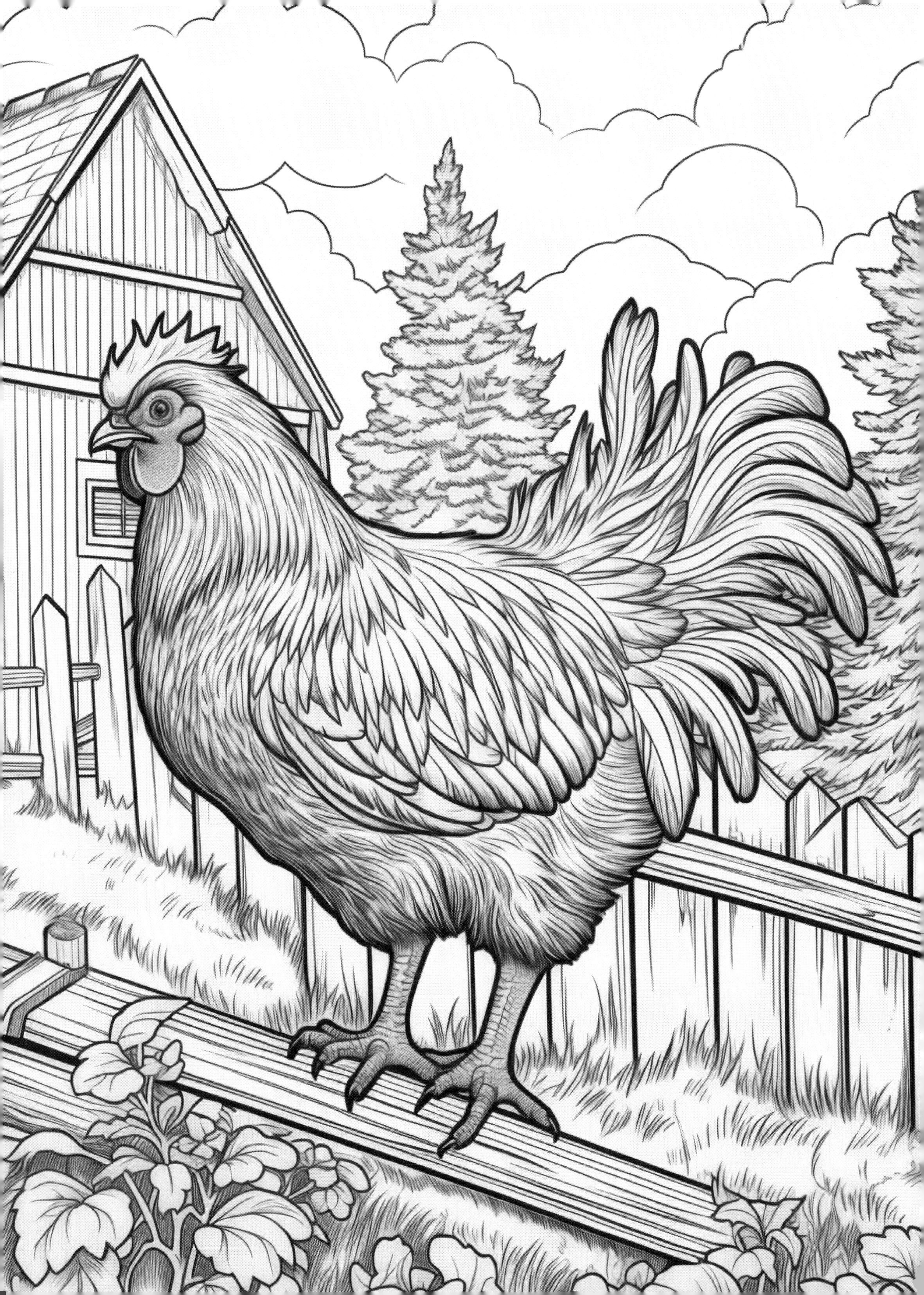

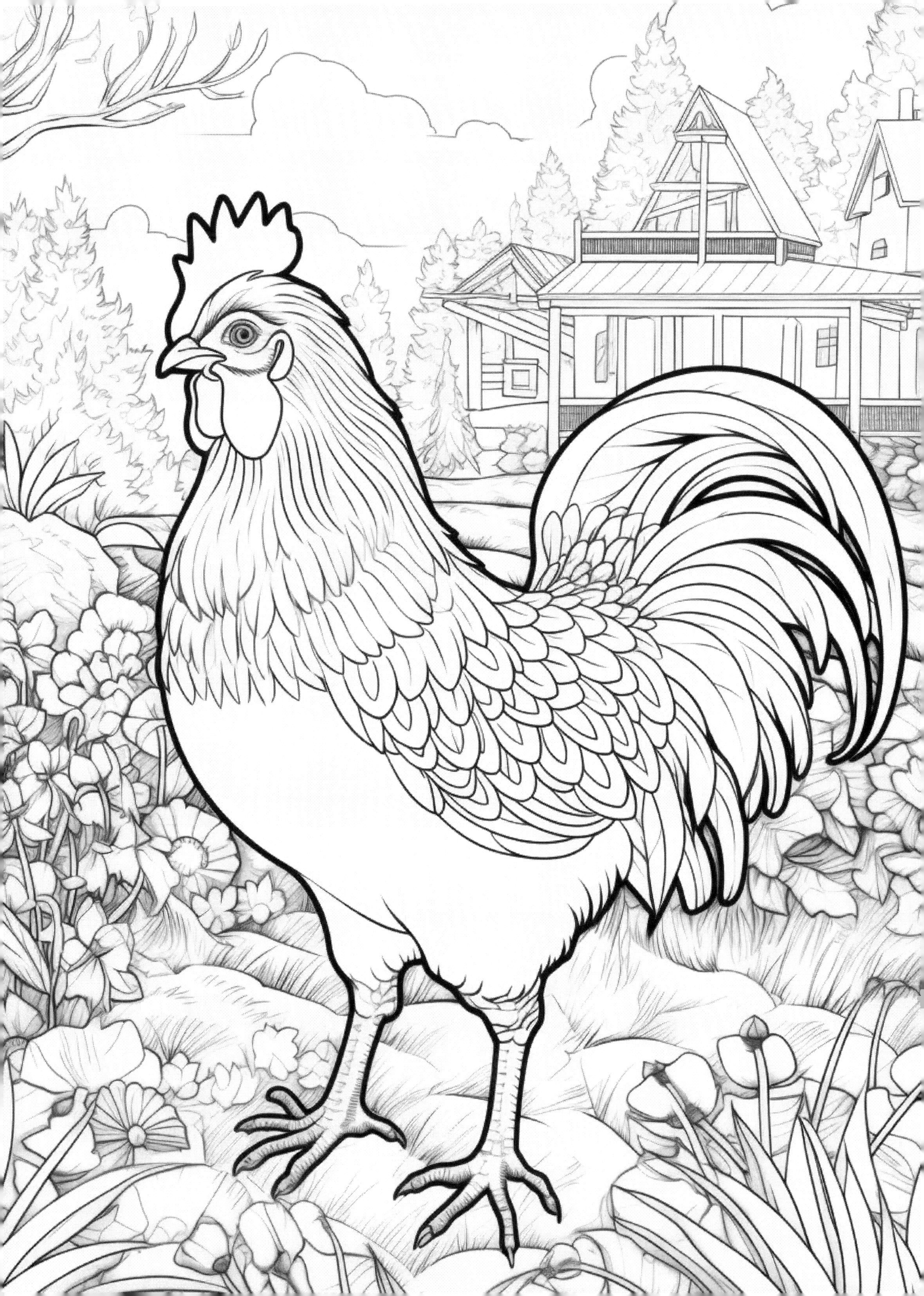

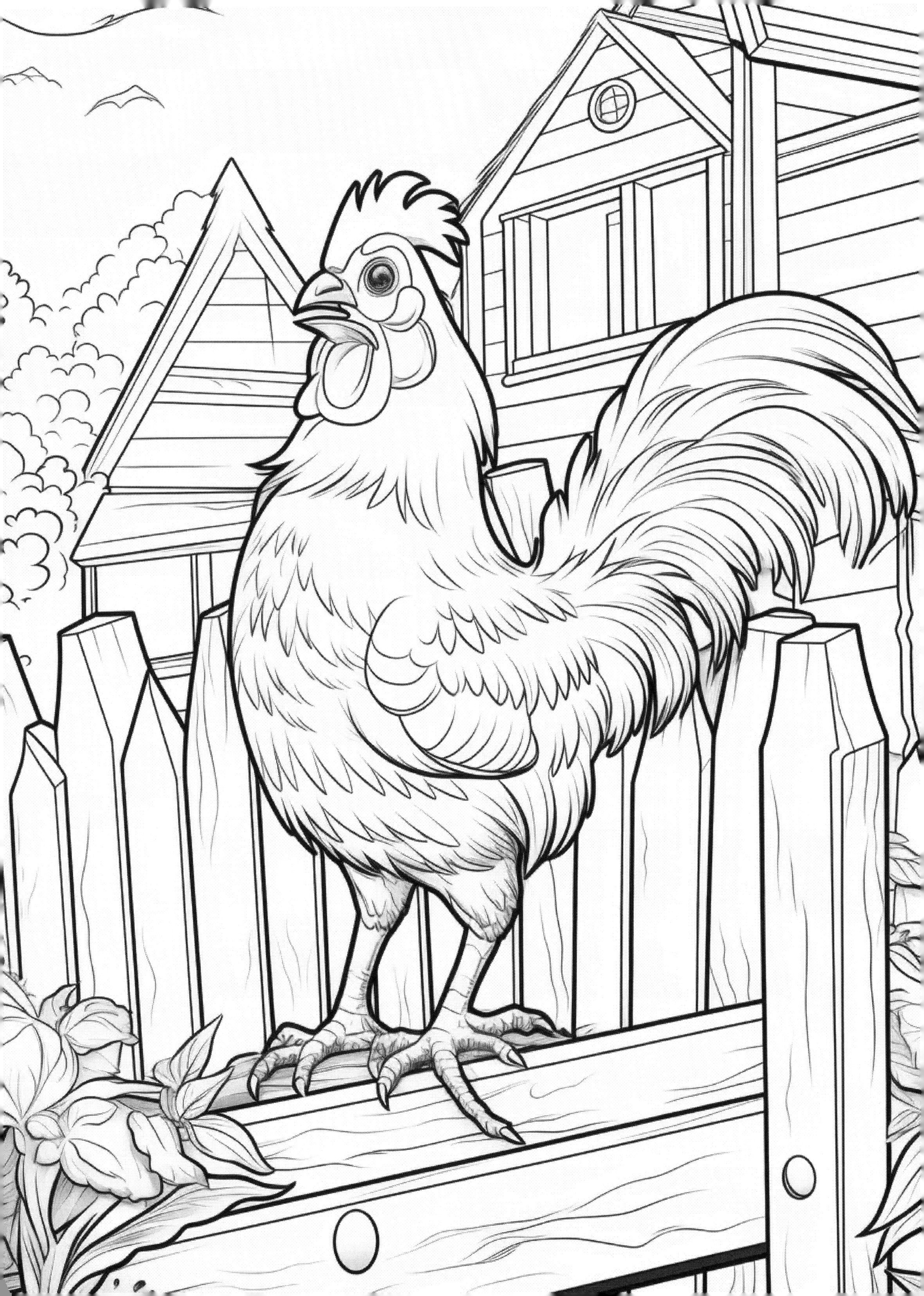

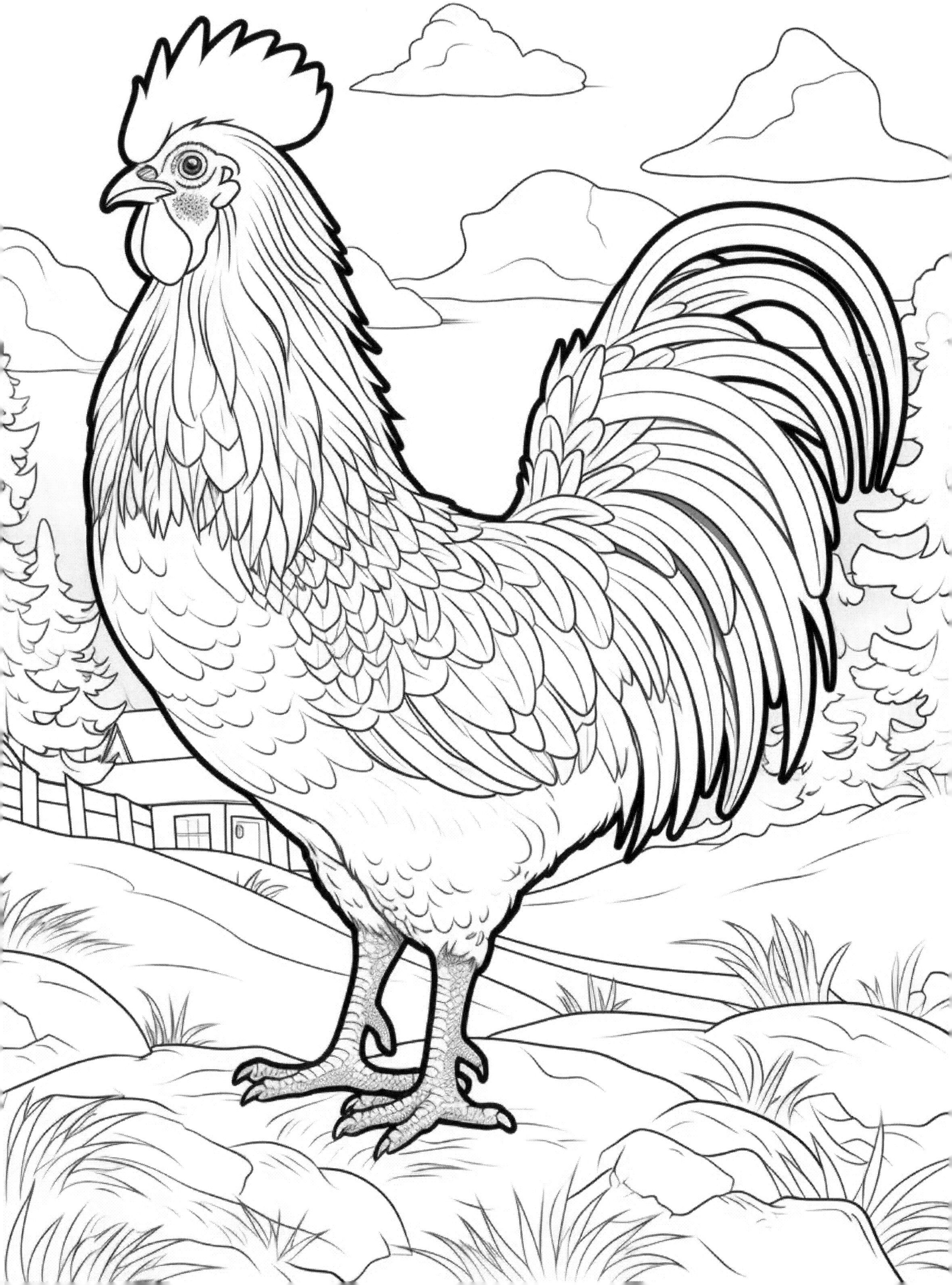

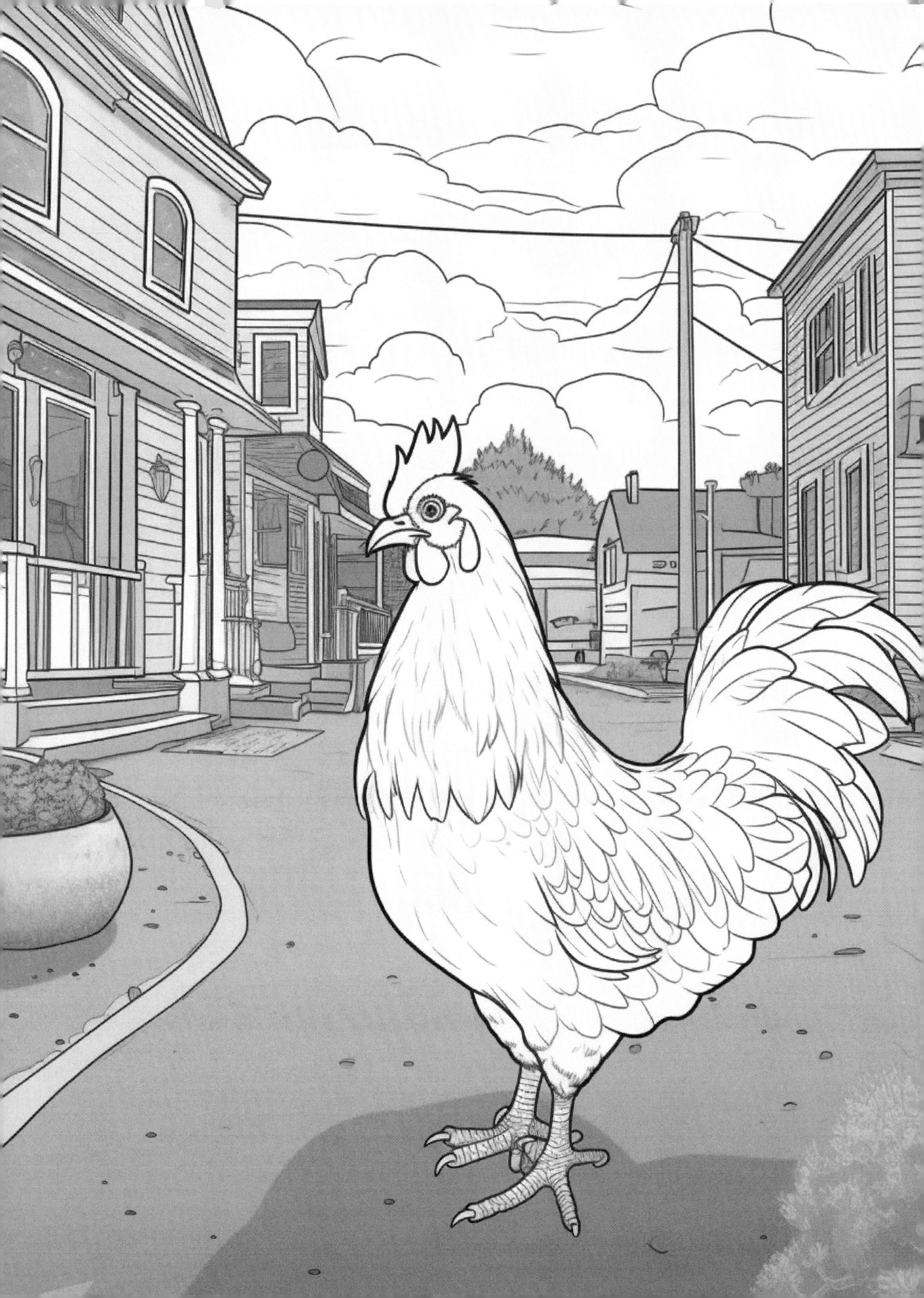

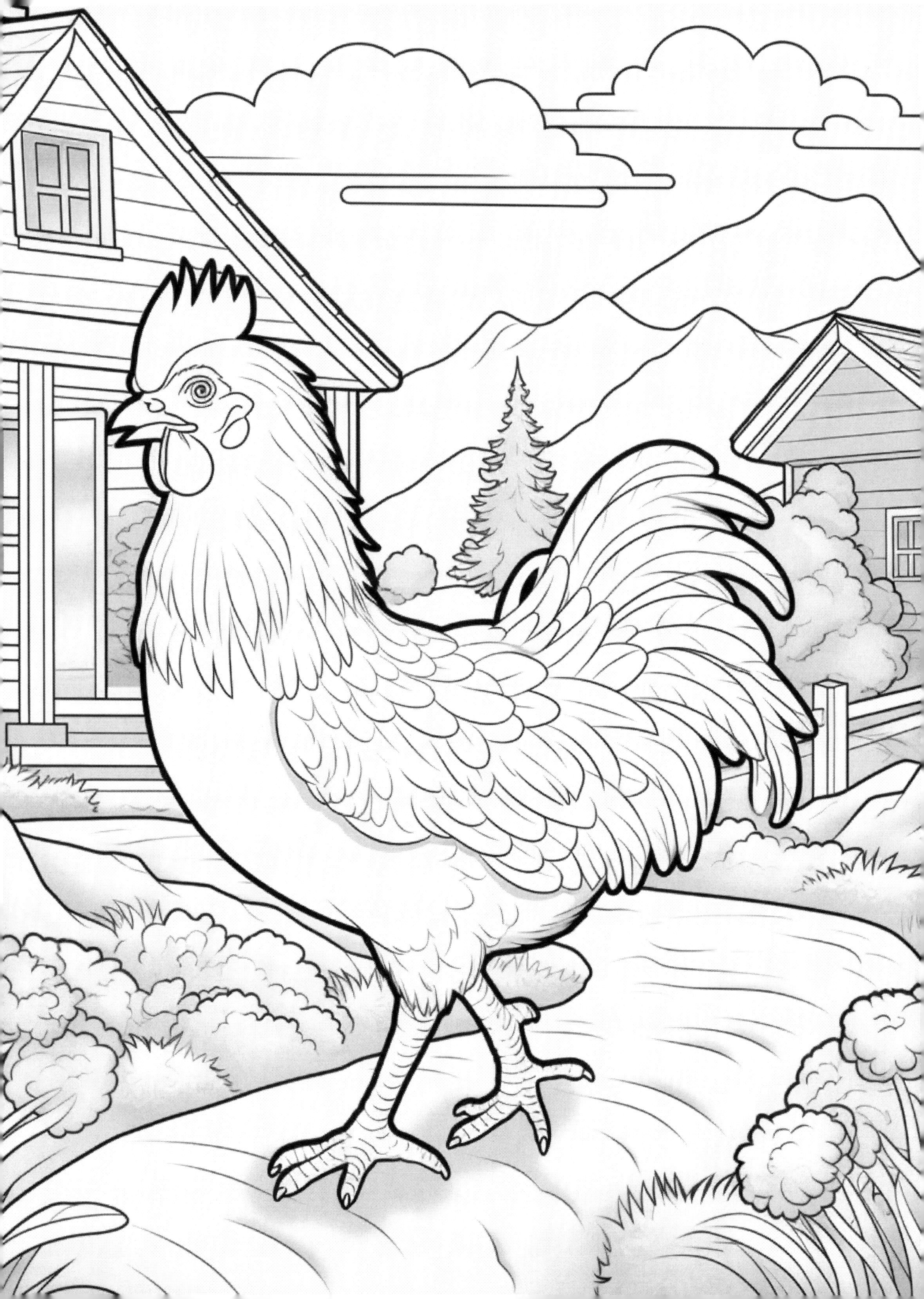

Copyright:
Christiano Mancini, c/o AutorenServices.de, Birkenallee 24, 36037 Fulda
Christiano.Mancini@gmx.de

ISBN:
979-8394388453

Made in the USA
Las Vegas, NV
19 December 2024

14768470R00037